NOW WHAT?

Real World Advice for Graduates

BOB VISOTCKY

Copyright © 2020 Bob Visotcky
All rights reserved
First Edition

PAGE PUBLISHING, INC.
Conneaut Lake, PA

First originally published by Page Publishing 2020

ISBN 978-1-64628-697-3 (pbk)
ISBN 978-1-64628-698-0 (digital)

Printed in the United States of America

This book is dedicated to my three amazing children: Demi, Johnny, and Sophia. The greatest joy I have in this life is watching these three amazing people grow into the outstanding human beings they have become.

Love you guys…

Dad

Contents

Foreword 11

My Journey 13
My Family 13
    Making Bruce Springsteen's "Born to Run" the State
    Theme Song of New Jersey in 1980 20
    You Never Know Who Is Sitting Next to You 24
Don't Ever Say I Can't Sell or I Don't Like Sales 25
If Money and Resources Weren't a Factor, Write Down
Everything You Want Out of Life 25
Find Your Why 26
What Is Your Passion? 26
Nobody Owes You Anything; Work for What You Want 27
Have Mentors for Every Aspect of Your Life 27
Proper Way to Greet Someone 27
The Job Search 28
    Finding the right job is a job in itself! 28
    Hire a professional résumé writer. 28
Steps for Job Search Preparation 28
    Dress for success. 30
Conference Room Meetings 30
Possible Interview Questions 31
    These Next Interviewing Questions Are Designed to
    See How You Answer Under Pressure 32
    Ask Your Potential Boss a Few Questions 32
Post-Interview/Handwritten Thank-You Note 33

Writer's Block 33
Negotiating Your Salary...33
Go Where You Are Wanted 34
Never Search for a Job Without a Job but There Are Exceptions!..34
Save 10% of Every Check and Possibly Retire in Your Forties.......36
Manage Your Addiction to Technology / Smartphones /
Video Games / Laptops / Tobacco and Alcohol 37
You Are Always Being Monitored....................................38
Don't Be Afraid to Ask for What You Want 38
Take a Bad Situation and Turn It into a Good One 39
Forgiveness Gene!..40
Have Self-Confidence...41
Recognize Big Chances to Make Huge Money 41
Being Cheap Is a Major Turn Off.....................................42
Don't Drink and Drive 43
Texting and Driving Makes a Horrible Mix.....................43
Never Drink in Excess at Company Functions 43
Remember People's Names 43
Networking Is a Must / Social Media...............................44
Hire Positive Attitudes and Never Surround Yourself with
Mediocrity 44
Don't Ever Say That's Not My Job to Your Boss..............45
Most People Are Followers, so if You Want to Stand Out,
Be a Leader...46
Always Be on Time/No Sacred Cows...............................46
Accept Responsibility No Matter How Difficult It Is......47
How Can You Make a Difference If You Do What
Everybody Else Is Doing!..49
Don't Ignore Life's Wake-Up Calls...................................50
Share What You Learn (Pay It Forward) 63
When Asked to Speak in Front of a Crowd, Are You
Excited or Scared? 64
Quitting Is the Easy Way Out 64
Be a Difference Maker..65
More on Mentors 65
Four Keys to Build Your Brand..67

Think Like an Owner 67
Be Known Before You Are Needed 68
Look for the Positives in People Before the Negatives 68
Be a Good Listener.. 69
Never Answer a Question If You Don't Know the Answer 69
Read Five Hours a Week (One Hour Per Day) 69
Don't Cheat in Golf or in Anything for that Matter 69
Player or Victim 70
Time Healer 70
Why Are We More Popular When We Are Dead?...................... 71
People Buy Anything for Two Reasons 71
Stand Up for Those Who Can't Stand Up for Themselves! 71
Don't Make Excuses, Find Solutions.. 73
Do the Things You Hate First.. 73
A Bad Decision Is Better Than Not Making One 74
Hire People that Have the Skills You Lack.................................. 74
How to Terminate an Employee 74
Never Bad-mouth Your Employer, Company, or Teammates 75
I Wouldn't Want Dennis Rodman on My Team 75
Be Memorable... 75
Dating.. 77
Don't Reward Bad Behavior or Undeserved Behavior 77
Don't Think About Marriage Until You Are Twenty-Five Plus 78
My Grandpa John's Advice 78
Take Family Vacations / Dinnertime 79
Never Take Your Family for Granted 79
Be Highly Optimistic 80
Scared Money Loses 80
Don't Worry About Things You Can't Control 81
A Ball Always Bounces Back Up When It Hits Bottom 81
Put End Dates on Yourself.. 81
Don't Talk About it… Do It!... 82
Get a Physical Checkup Every Year at the Same Time.................. 82
Handle One Task at a Time/Prioritization 82
Timing Is Everything!.. 83
Save For Your Retirement 83

Do Your Taxes on Time and Hire an Accountant..........................83
Do One Major Experience That Gets You Out of Your
Comfort Zone Every Year..84
Buy Real Estate 85
Recurring Revenue Stream Businesses Are Best..........................86
Make Friends with the Biggest Guy in the Room 86
Being Stubborn Can Possibly Get You Killed 86
Tell Your Children to Introduce Themselves to Their
Teachers the First Day of Class 87
Be Creative...88
Your Mom..88
Write a Letter to Each of Your Children the Day They
Were Born and Read it at Their Wedding..................................88
Teach Your Children Manners...88
Communicate with Your Children Regularly.............................89
Let Your Kids Live Their Own Lives..89
Get Out of Debt 89
Buy What You Need Not What You Want................................90
Write Handwritten Personal Cards to Your Family and Friends....90
There Is Always Light at the End of the Tunnel........................90
You Aren't Always Right 90
Go with Your Gut Instincts 91
Don't Look for Perfection in an Imperfect World 91
Enjoy Your Job..91
Unemployment..92
Action Is the Cure for Procrastination 92
Love Yourself First 92
Don't Let Other People Define You Or Your Company.............93
Have an Open Mind and Be Flexible 93
Dieting Is a Temporary Fix...93
Kids Want Hang Time 94
Say Yes to Networking Opportunities.......................................94
There Is No Substitute for Hard Work 94
Selling Begins with the Word No 95

Integrity Is Everything! 95
    Story Number One 95
    Story Number Two 96
Sit on Major Decisions for Twenty-Four Hours 97
Your Business Card Can Make You Stand Out 98
Never Let Anyone Get in the Way of Your Career 98
Do Volunteer Work 99
Show Up Every Day 99
Learn From the Past, Don't Live In It and Embrace Change 100
How Would You Like to Be Remembered? 100

Foreword

So you just graduated from college or high school, or you have decided school just isn't for you, so it's time to put your big-boy or big-girl pants on! I have interviewed hundreds of people in your position and have spoken at college campuses, and it shocks me to see how unprepared students are for the real world.

I went to college too, but I went to class in a suit and tie and made sales calls for two local radio stations in Morgantown, West Virginia—WAJR and WVAQ—in between classes. On weekends, I traveled an hour to my DJ job at WANB in Waynesburg, Pennsylvania. I worked seven days a week and went to college full-time. That's how bad I wanted a career in radio!

Believe it or not, I found time to have my fun too. I was an active member of Phi Kappa Psi Fraternity at West Virginia University (WVU); a campaign manager for Junior Taylor, who ran for student body president; and was the WVU Mountaineer school mascot.

This book will give you the advice I wish I had before I graduated. If you actually do some of the tasks I suggest, I promise you will have an excellent chance at being successful, not only in your job but financially as well! So sit back, relax, and enjoy the read!

Thank you for taking the first step to success…

My Journey

For the past forty years, I have worked in radio, TV, print, outdoor, digital, and owned my own business—which was a product for the real estate industry—called the Listinglight, a night-light for real estate signs. We sold twenty thousand units in seven countries, and the Listinglight was named one of the "Best Innovative Tech Inventions of the Year" by *REALTOR Magazine* in 2007. My family and I have lived in seven of the top ten markets as well as some medium and small markets. I have been in senior-level management since age thirty and have many life lessons and stories to share with you, so here we go!

My Family

Let me start by saying, I loved my dad, but we had a love-hate relationship. You see, he was always right, and I was always wrong, and that equation didn't work for me. I have learned many great things from my father, but I wanted to fill in the blanks that I have learned along the way and always feel I'm learning new things daily.

The good news was that my dad gave me the edge to succeed and taught my brother and I respect. I always had to prove my dad wrong, so when someone says I can't do something, that just gives me more motivation to succeed!

My brother, Rich, and I grew up in a small town in Garfield, New Jersey, with roughly thirty-five thousand people in Bergen

County. It's about thirty minutes from New York City without traffic and 1 hour with traffic! My father was a politician and lived it 24-7. It seems that we were always going at it constantly, and the tiniest things would set him off. I guess I was a rebel and hated authority, but I did love him and respected him. (*Lesson: If you don't like the person, respect their title.*)

Deep down, I knew my dad loved me. He just had a shitty way of showing it. He worked hard as a meter reader for Public Service in Passaic, New Jersey, during the day and was a politician…always. He worked his way up from county committeeman to city councilman, mayor of Garfield, New Jersey, Deputy Speaker of the state assembly for the thirty-sixth district in New Jersey. I know he loved my brother and me, but I guess I needed more attention than I received. It seemed politics was more important than family, and I resented it. My brother, on the other hand, loved politics, but I hated the bullshit of party politics. My dad's daily regiment would be wake up at 6:30 a.m., throw up, take a shower, go to work, come home, take a fifteen-minute nap, yell at me for something, eat dinner, and then go politicking until 2:00 or 3:00 a.m. He smoked too much and drank too much, and those were great lessons because my brother and I never touched a cigarette. We are social drinkers and maybe smoke an occasional cigar but not abusers. (*Lesson: Don't drink or smoke in excess.*)

I hated when I read about politician's kids getting in trouble for drugs or alcohol, and I made a promise to my dad that I would never do drugs, smoke cigarettes, or embarrass the family as long as he never got indicted…LOL. I was proud to be a Visotcky and felt my reputation was everything. What I learned later, as a father, was, he was making money to support our family. With his political checks, he automatically sent it to our private schools and paid tuition. I don't think I ever properly thanked my mom and dad for making that sacrifice, but I totally understand now, and you will, too, when you have children. Both my parents are gone now, but I want to say, "Thank you for all you have done for me. You were great parents and made me the man I am today."

NOW WHAT?

Warren Beatty said it best. "You'll never know how great it is to have a child until you actually have one."

The lesson here is, *your parents are excellent role models if you let them.*

My mom, Lois; Grandma Edee; and Grandpa John were all my heroes. They loved me unconditionally, and I spent more time at my grandparents' house than my own. I would get into brutal verbal fighting matches with my dad and run to my grandparents' house, crying. I named my son after my Grandpa Johnny, and my youngest daughter's middle name is Lois after my mom. We used to sit on my grandparents' front porch for hours and rocked and talked about everything. I miss my grandparents, mom, and dad and think about them every day.

One day, me and my grandma were in the grocery store, and I ran the cart right into her heels. Most grandparents would yell, scream, and give you a lecture. I could clearly see the pain she was experiencing but just sucked it up and knew that I did not do that intentionally. She taught me to be calm in difficult situations. She could have easily blown up at me, but look, it's over forty-eight years later, and I still remember that lesson.

My grandfather was my hero! I had a paper route with eighty-one customers, and if it were raining, he would drive the car while I delivered all my papers. We spent almost every day after school, either bowling, fishing, or just sitting on his front porch. My Grandma Edee was a saint, and I loved her dearly. She sent cards to everyone for every occasion, and the lesson here is, *write handwritten thank-you notes. Don't forget birthdays and anniversaries, etc.*

As I write this book, it's been over two years since we lost my mom (June 25, 2017). She was the best mom a kid could ask for. The reason my mom was so great was she had great parents that stayed married and loved us unconditionally. My mom passed that trait on to my brother and me except my brother and I both had two marriages…LOL. She always put her kids first and sacrificed everything for us. She never had a lot of money but would always surprise us with big checks on our birthdays.

Here are two very memorable moments from my mom, and there were many more. I was watching TV when I was about six years old one early afternoon and lunch was ready, but I wasn't. My mom repeatedly ordered me to the table, and I ignored her. She then burst into the living room and hit me on the head with a felt potholder. What she didn't realize was the fact that the potholder had a magnet that was usually used to attach to the refrigerator, but the magnet totally cut my head open, and she was devastated. I wasn't mad. My grandfather came to the rescue, and I actually thought to myself, *What were the odds that a potholder could cause stitches?*

The other main event was during lunch at our house at 9 Pershing Street in Garfield, New Jersey. My dad always sat at the head of the table, but when he wasn't around, I sat there because I was a rebel. The stove was directly to the right of me, and my mom was about to light the pilot light. The problem was the gas was so high that it blew up, and my mom jumped in front of the stove so I wouldn't get burned. She suffered second and third-degree burns on her face, and she will always be my hero. She had a split second to react, and she did.

My brother, Rich, was a huge role model. He joined the Garfield Volunteer Ambulance Corps first, and I followed. He went to West Virginia University, and I followed. He was a member of the Phi Kappa Psi, and I followed. He is like my mom, and I am like my dad. Skip, that's my brother's nickname, is book smart, and I am street-smart. He became a lawyer, and I ran radio stations all over the country. I have always looked up to my brother, and we talk on the phone every day even though we live on opposite coasts.

I joined Garfield, New Jersey, Volunteer Ambulance Corps when I was fifteen, but you needed to be sixteen…Shhhh! Until this day, that was the best job I ever had, and it was 100% volunteer. Helping others is an amazing feeling, and trying to save someone's life is a huge responsibly I didn't take lightly. (*Give back to the community whenever you can.*)

I hung out, most of my free time, at the Garfield Volunteer Ambulance Corps and worked at a small grocery store called Emil's Foodtown in my teen years. My bosses, Alan and Gary, were great guys at the grocery store, and they trusted me. I never violated their trust, and that job taught me a lot on how to be a leader, and I was only seventeen. They made me a night manager and had thirty-plus-year-old's reporting to me. When I graduated from Paramus Catholic High School, I got accepted to WVU and wanted to become a doctor or radio announcer. Getting a *D* in Biology 1 and a head-on car collision in November of my freshman year basically extinguished my chances of becoming a doctor.

Now it's off to radio! Cousin Brucie on 77 WABC New York City was my childhood radio hero, and at age seven, I told my brother and Grandpa I will work at WABC one day. Oddly enough, when I turned twenty-two, I was working at WABC's sister station on the FM band, WPLJ, and Cousin Brucie worked one floor below me. I met Cousin Brucie once at a radio carnival in Manhattan and thanked him for inspiring me to have a career in the radio industry. I had no fear during my college years at West Virginia University, and the word *no* wasn't in my vocabulary. So my junior year, I walked into the West Virginia Radio Corporation studios in Morgantown, West Virginia, where they owned WAJR/WVAQ and met with the news director, Hoppy Kercheval. I asked Hoppy for an internship, and he said he wasn't interested. (*Selling begins with the word no.*)

Hoppy said, "If you find me a story that nobody else has, I might give you a shot."

A few hours later, I returned with a scoop on dirty rush tactics by the Chi Omega Sorority House at WVU, and Hoppy hired me as an intern in the news department. Hoppy and I became great friends and actually were roommates my junior and senior year. We were reunited at West Virginia Radio Corporation forty years later, Hoppy; Dale Miller, now President of West Virginia Radio and me. Guess it all comes around? I would be remiss not to mention one of the best owners and class acts I have ever met, is John Raese, the owner of West Virginia Radio Corporation and Greer Industries. John also is a dead look-alike ringer for my older brother, Rich. You can't call him Skip unless you were family!

Getting back to my first newscasts at WAJR, let me just say my on-air performance sucked, probably due to excessive drinking and getting up at 3:00 a.m. to get the news! One Saturday morning, Dale Miller, the Vice President / General Manager at the time, and Hoppy walked into the newsroom after my disaster newscast, and Dale said, "What was that?"

Dale explained to me that everyone has a niche, and I seem to know everyone in town, so why don't I sell for them? I told Dale I didn't go to college to be a salesman, but boy did it work out for me in the long run. I wore a suit and tie to class and sold airtime in-between classes. The beauty was that I never had to ask my dad or mom for money, but one thing I'll always remember was that my dad wasn't cheap. He always picked up the tab whenever we were together, and unfortunately, that is one lesson from him I need to stop...LOL. (*Don't be cheap.*)

I loved my sales job at West Virginia Radio Corporation but wanted to work for a major market radio station after graduation. My sights were set on New York City, Chicago, or Los Angeles, and everyone said that would never happen. Believe me, when someone says I can't do something, that's all I need to hear. My dad, let's just say, wasn't too encouraging, and during his entire life, I just kept doing things he thought I couldn't such as running the New York City Marathon in 1986, being a certified scuba diver at the Great Barrier Reef in Australia, jumping out of a perfectly good airplane, becoming a general manager of a radio station, owning a 450SL Mercedes convertible, building my own home, etc., all by the age of thirty.

I actually was quite a good bowler before college and probably could have qualified for the Professional Bowlers Tour, but my dad insisted I go to college, so I hung up my bowling ball and shoes and followed my brother, Rich, to West Virginia University. My mother actually thought I was a drug dealer because I won so much money bowling and hustling older guys who thought they could beat me.

I canceled my spring break trip to Fort Lauderdale, Florida, my senior year in 1979 and drove 7 1/2 hours to Manhattan to pitch three sales jobs: WPLJ-FM, WCBS-FM, and the Katz Rep Firm. WCBS-FM said they would hire me late in the summer after graduation. Katz wasn't interested, and the General Sales Manager at

NOW WHAT?

WPLJ-FM, Larry Divney, told me to see him when I graduated in May, and he would find me a job in New York City. I trusted this man, and my gut is always right, so one of my first lessons to graduates or anyone else is to *trust your gut instincts.*

Oh, I forgot to mention. I pitched a sales job for a small local station called WOMB in New Jersey, and they didn't hire me. The joy I had when I called the sales manager to let him know the number one best rock station in New York City, WPLJ, hired me!

Let me back up for a minute. I'll never forget meeting with my boss in West Virginia, Dale Miller, the President and CEO of West Virginia Radio Corporation. I took him to lunch and told him I was resigning basically without a job. He initially laughed but not in you-are-crazy-in-a-stupid way but in a crazy-you-probably-will-pull-it-off way! Dale believed in me, and we are still good friends today. We worked together forty years later, running his Charleston radio cluster, and Hoppy was my roommate in Charleston, West Virginia, when he covered the legislature down in Charleston. (*Don't burn bridges!*)

So I graduated from WVU on May 21, 1979, and went to meet Larry Divney, WPLJ's General Sales Manager, the following Monday. Larry explained to me that Nick Trigony is the President / General Manager of WPLJ, and if I meet with him and he likes me, WPLJ may have an account executive position for me! I was beyond the moon! So I left Larry's office and walked into this huge corner office at 1330 Avenue of the Americas to meet Nick Trigony and fell over his glass coffee table upon entry right on my ass. Great first impression, but they hired me there for 3 1/2 years and then WLS for 3 1/2 years and KTKS for one year all within the ABC Owned and Operated Radio Stations. One of the reasons I'm writing this book is what happened next.

This was the late 70s. Our family didn't have a lot of money. My mom, was a stay-at-home mom at the time, and my dad was always busy with politics. He worked really hard during the day as a meter reader for Public Service Electric and Gas in Passaic, New Jersey.

My first day at my new job, I walked into WPLJ at 54th and 6th in Midtown Manhattan with four-inch disco platform heels, a plaid sport coat, and a tie that didn't match. I was the Herb Tarleck of WPLJ. For you younger readers, WKRP Cincinnati was a huge TV hit show, and the character, Herb Tarleck, was an abrasive bad dresser in charge of sales. The girls in the office laughed at me, but our local sales manager, Marc Morgan, and General Manager, Nick Trigony, both said they would help me find suits and ties, and that's when I said, *"These are things I wish I knew before I entered the real world."*

I read many self-help books and realized to dress for the job you want, not the job you have! One really cool thing was I parked in the lot right next door to Studio 54 in its heyday and walked pass that scene every night. The bouncers picked who they wanted to let in, and when a limo pulled up with a bunch of hot models, the bouncers always let them in! You had to have the right look to get in.

Making Bruce Springsteen's "Born to Run" the State Theme Song of New Jersey in 1980

In 1980, my dad did a really cool thing for me and our radio station, WPLJ New York City. The State of New Jersey was looking for a state theme song. So one night, my mom, dad, brother, and I were playing cards in our dining room, listening to the Carol Miller show, the nighttime DJ at WPLJ. She was a huge Bruce Springsteen fan, and during a "talk break," she said on-air, "Wouldn't it be cool for New Jersey to name 'Born to Run' the state theme song of New Jersey?"

Now my brother says he told dad to put the bill in the state assembly, but I honestly don't remember if it was he or I. It doesn't matter.

My dad looked at me and said, "Son, if I do this, would it help you?"

I told him, "Absolutely." He also asked me for the words of the song and told him not to worry about the words just please introduce the resolution…LOL. "This town rips the bones from your back, it's a death trap it's a suicide rap" probably wouldn't have gone over too well if I told him…LOL.

So he put the bill in motion!

NOW WHAT?

Here I am, a twenty-two-year-old working at one of the largest rock stations in the country, and we are about to make international news! I went to work the next day and ran into Larry Berger's office who was the Program Director and told him my dad will adopt a bill to make "Born to Run" the state theme song for New Jersey.

Larry didn't love salespeople, but I think he liked me and was thrilled to hear the news! Everyone at the station went crazy, especially Carol Miller, who is a gorgeous human being inside and out. Since I was in the radio business, radio stations from all over the country wanted an interview with my dad and me!

Long story short, we had a write-in promotion at WPLJ, and Carol Miller and I brought 250,000 postcards from people all over New Jersey, telling the legislators to make "Born to Run" the state theme song. We lost the official title, but "Born to Run" became the unofficial State Rock Theme Song of New Jersey, and it helped us get better ratings in New Jersey.

One of my thrills was riding in a limo with Carol Miller to the state capital in New Jersey in Trenton and back to present those postcards to the New Jersey State Assembly. The limo driver actually fell asleep in the Lincoln Tunnel on the ride home and hit the side of the tunnel, but nobody was hurt.

Here is a copy of the actual resolution:

> WHEREAS, Bruce Springsteen, who was born in 1949 in Freehold, Monmouth county and grew up amid the friendly, tranquil, small-town atmosphere that exists in that historic county seat, and who came to know well in his youth the sights, sounds and styles of summer life on the beach and boardwalk of that nearby ocean resort town of Asbury Park, today is recognized as one of pop music's most talented and outstanding performers, as well as one of its most influential and innovative artists; and

BOB VISOTCKY

WHEREAS, Bruce Springsteen, through his special ability to trans-form his experiences and environments, many of them framed and shaped by his youthful years as a resident of the State of New Jersey, into vivid musical compositions, and in his unique fusion of the diverse traditions of rock music, percussion productions and urban rhythm and blues, has touched a universal chord of music, experience and life-force among today's youth; and

WHEREAS, Bruce Springsteen's talents as a singer-songwriter, from his debut album, Greetings From Asbury Park, N. J., through his dramatically detailed soul and Latin-tinged album, The Wild, The Innocent and the E Street Shuffle, and in his galvanic album, Born to Run, whose title song has achieved anthem-like status throughout the world and has been adopted as their song by the teenagers of New Jersey; and

WHEREAS, Bruce Springsteen's live performances, particularly with his E Street Band, have been hailed as the most exciting shows on the world concert circuit, in which this young musician's seemingly unlimited energies and enthusiasm, plus his genuine modesty and honest concern for providing his faithful audiences with a performance they deserve, all serve to enhance his well earned reputation as New Jersey's Pop Music Ambassador to America; now, therefore,

BE IT RESOLVED by the General Assembly of the State of New Jersey (the Senate concurring):

1. That this Legislature salutes the outstanding musical talents, abilities and achievements of Bruce Springsteen; pays tribute to

his preeminent status as an artist and performer; commends him for providing entertainment, enlightenment and enrichment to peoples throughout the world; expresses its appreciation for the recognition which he has brought to the State of New Jersey; wishes him continued success and fulfillment in his career.
2. That thus Legislature declares *[Bruce Springsteen to be the New Jersey Pop Music Ambassador to America and calls upon the young people of all ages throughout New Jersey to adopt his songs] * "Born to Run" as the unofficial *rock* theme of our State's youth.
3. That a duly authenticated copy of this resolution signed by the President of the Senate and attested by the Secretary thereof and signed by the Speaker and attested by the Cleric of the General Assembly, be presented to Bruce Springsteen.

The resolution passed the Assembly on June 12, 1980, by voice vote. But it never made it through the state Senate, presumably because the senators listened to the lyrics and realized that the song is about a desire to get out of New Jersey.

The song was actually about teenage independence, but what do Senators know anyway?

My dad passed away on November 2nd, 2002, and six months before he died, we had a major heart-to-heart, and I asked him why he was so mean to me at times when I was growing up. He told me he couldn't get angry with his constituents, but I was an easy target. We both cried, hugged, and I was set free! My father never admitted to ever being wrong until that day. I wanted to hear that all my life, and it finally happened. (*Lesson: Admit when you are wrong and don't hold grudges.*)

You Never Know Who Is Sitting Next to You

My dad loved this local bar in Garfield, New Jersey, called Koby's Tavern. You see, in Garfield, there was a bar on almost every street corner, but this was a special place. When my mom told my dad to spend time with his son, he would bring me to Koby's. The problem was he'd tell me to wait in the car while he got a pack of cigarettes and that would take two to three hours.

On my eighteenth birthday, my best friend, Sal Spoto, and I went for a drink at Koby's, and we both knew the owner Mr. Kobylarz very well, and we began to drink. My father was Mayor of Garfield at the time, and the guy sitting next to me had no idea who I was and was popping off on how shitty my dad was as Mayor of Garfield.

My best friend, Sal, is a big dude and was ready to break the guy's neck, but I wanted the guy to keep on going, so I said to the man, "You really hate the mayor, don't you?"

He replied, "Yes, sir!"

I quietly whispered into his ear that the mayor is my father. The guy didn't know what to do. He broke out in a sweat, bought Sal and I a drink, and left the premises immediately. The look on that guy's face was worth everything to me because I learned two valuable lessons that day. (*Be careful what you say in public, and it's better not to get angry because he felt worst the way I handled it.*)

I was married for five years to my college sweetheart, got divorced, took five years off, and then married my second wife, Secia, who together, we raised three of the best children on the planet: Demi, Johnny, and Sophia. We stayed married for twenty-five years, and then she married her old boyfriend very soon after the divorce. I can't give you much advice on staying married, but I know unconditional love is out there, and it is very hard to find. When you find it, don't let it pass you by.

NOW WHAT?

Don't Ever Say I Can't Sell or I Don't Like Sales

Here's a news flash. You are always selling, so stop saying, "I can't!" First impressions are everything and most times, you only have one chance to make an impression, so don't spoil it. We are constantly selling, so don't sell yourself short. Dress for the job you want, not the job you have. You don't have to love sales but don't kid yourself, if you go to a job interview, you are selling yourself.

If Money and Resources Weren't a Factor, Write Down Everything You Want Out of Life

Seriously, if you write down the things you want to happen, they will! By writing things down you've taken an intangible and made it a tangible.

Go into a quiet room or library, and close your eyes, and think, *If money and resources were no object, what do I want out of my life?* The key is once you write them down, look at it every month, and cross out the ones you have accomplished. On December 15, write down all your goals, and start the following year with the goals that you haven't achieved yet.

When I was twenty-two, I wrote down I wanted to be a radio station general manager, have my own home, and have a 450SL convertible Mercedes Benz in my garage by my thirtieth birthday! On my thirtieth birthday, I was General Manager at 103.5 The Fox in Denver; had a brand-new house built in Evergreen, Colorado; and a black 450SL Mercedes Benz in my garage. It works...try it today! If you make a list every year, I promise you will cross things out and have new goals. If you don't write things down, the chances of you achieving what you truly desire probably will never happen. Without a plan, you are flying an airplane without any instruments. Dream with your eyes open so you can see what you want!

Find Your Why

Simon Sinek recently wrote a book on "Starting With Why," which is fascinating and so true. We always tell an employer what we did and how we did it but never why we do what we do. The question you need to ask yourself is, Why should people hire you? Sinek goes on to say that answering the "why" is the decision part of the brain. So when you go to an interview, ask yourself why they need you and your service instead of what and how great you are.

One of my bosses, Mike Glickenhaus, gave me a recommendation that stated, "Bob is a difference maker."

That is probably the nicest compliment I have ever received. Making a difference in someone's life or company to me is priceless, and I believe I left a part of me at every media outlet I was lucky enough to be employed at. Who doesn't want an employee that makes a difference in its organization?

What Is Your Passion?

What would you love to wake up to do every morning? Is it acting, playing music, playing your favorite sport, selling, teaching, etc.? Once you identify your passion, go after it and never look back!

I'm not saying do just one thing. You should be open to new opportunities as well. Jack Nicklaus was arguably the best golfer of all time and said that he exposed his children to all sports, not just golf so they can find their own passion. I personally tried everything and found out that radio, entertaining, speaking, and playing golf were my favorite passions, but I'm actually very passionate about writing this book and sharing what I have learned along the way!

My son, Johnny, called me and said he was dropping out of the University of Arizona after one semester to pursue acting. My answer probably surprised him, but I said, "Johnny, go follow your passion and dreams." Today, Johnny is living his dream and acting in Los Angeles.

NOW WHAT?

Nobody Owes You Anything; Work for What You Want

Having a great work ethic will get you places! The only person you need to rely on is yourself, so don't expect handouts and special favors from people. Those things will come if you work hard and show your worth to your employers.

A person once came into my office and said they'd like to pitch the next management position that becomes available. My response was, "You are pitching that job every day you show up at work."

Management is always watching and learning about you. They know everything that's going on in the office too, so don't hide an in-office romance or anything else you might have divulged to another employee. As a manager for a very long time, there are very few secrets that slipped by me.

Have Mentors for Every Aspect of Your Life

- · Find the best financial adviser.
- · Find the best business coach.
- · Find the best relationship specialist.
- · Find the best partner to share your life with.

Most of all, don't forget your parents! Your parents have your best interests at heart and have tons of life experiences you can learn from. Millennials don't seem to understand that quite yet. You seem to add more weight to your friends rather than your parents, and that's a major mistake!

Proper Way to Greet Someone

This is such a simple exercise, but you'd be surprised how many people get it wrong. *Smile*, extend your hand to meet theirs, look them in the eye, and meet their grip pressure. If you squeeze too tightly, it shows superiority, too light shows weakness, but the same pressure shows you are making a bond.

I usually say, "Hi, my name is Bob Visotcky. What's yours?" Then I start a brief conversation that fits the greeting. Smiling and having a positive attitude is everything, so smile more, and frown less.

The Job Search

Finding the right job is a job in itself!

Being in the radio and the media industry is a very tough business, and staying at one radio station is nearly impossible. I moved over fifteen times and have worked in New York City, Chicago, Dallas, Philadelphia, Denver, Cleveland, San Diego, San Francisco, Los Angeles, Grand Junction, and West Virginia. Not only did I have to find a job but also find a home and make sure the kids were taken care of with schools, etc. Moving is tough, but you have to weigh all your options before taking the leap.

Hire a professional résumé writer.

Sure, there are programs on your computer that are okay, but a professional knows what keywords to add that will get a recruiter's attention.
    Investigate a company that you want to work for before you send a résumé. Go to their website, LinkedIn, Instagram, Snapchat, or Facebook page. You may know an employee that works there. See if they support a charity you are familiar with. If all else fails, ask to speak to a salesperson. Salespeople have big mouths, and you can find out just about anything going on at a company by speaking to a salesperson.

Steps for Job Search Preparation

What companies and jobs will make you excited to come to work everyday?

1. The first key is to wake up early, just like you are going to work. Dress up because you won't be disappointed once

you find a job that you already are dressing like you had a job. Make your bed before you leave for the day because at least that's one task you accomplished and can lead to many more throughout the day.
2. Visit the company's website and see if there is anyone you know or a common charity you both support.
3. Go to LinkedIn and see if there are people you know that work there so they can introduce you to the right people.
4. Make friends with the gatekeeper you are trying to get an appointment with. My trick is, I say my name and ask if they are the owner.
They often laugh, and they say, "I wish."
Then I ask them their name and say, "I need your help."
Bingo…try it. It works!
5. Visit the business, and see how people are interacting with each other before the interview if possible.
6. Deliver your résumé in person.
I love it when a gatekeeper tries to set up a roadblock and asks, "Do you have an appointment?"
I always say with a huge smile, "No, but that's why I'm here. I wanted to put a face to my résumé!"
I have interviewed hundreds of people in my radio career, and I love when someone shows up at the front door and asks to meet with me. Nine times out of ten, I will make time because I appreciate the effort. Trust me, there are a lot of asshole bosses out there that think their shit doesn't stink, and you don't want to work for those people.
7. If you are granted an interview, ask how many people will be in the meeting, and make sure you have color copies for all, and make sure all the names are spelled correctly.
8. Explain why they need to hire you as well as how and what you have achieved thus far.

Dress for success.

First impressions are everything and very seldom do you get a second chance. Check yourself in the mirror when you leave the house and say, "Do I want to do business with me today?"

I worked with Debbie Payne, the classiest account executive at KABC Radio Los Angeles. She sold for us, and one day, I asked her, "Why do you always dress up and look so good even in casual settings?" Back then a simple compliment like that wasn't considered sexual harassment but in today's "me too" movement, I suggest you be careful on how you compliment anyone in the workplace.

She smiled and replied, "You'll never know who you're going to meet."

A potential sales candidate came to my office in Charleston, West Virginia, and wanted a sales job. He was dressed, let's call it, less than business casual. After two minutes, I asked him why he didn't wear a suit and tie, and what does he know about our radio stations.

He turned pitch red and confessed, "Not much."

I told him if he seriously wanted to work for me, come back and let me know it!

The first interview lasted two minutes! He came back the next day dressed in a suit and tie and knew more info on the stations than I did. I hired him, and he worked out very well. The reason he got a second chance is because I knew he cared and was upset with himself. That's another reason I'm writing this book. *He wasn't shown the way by anyone!*

Conference Room Meetings

If you are meeting in a conference room, ask the person you are meeting with where they'd like you to sit. If you have to hook up a computer, get there earlier, and ask the receptionist the best way to set up your computer.

I had a girl walk into my office at KLOS in Los Angeles and had a professional presentation on her iPad, and it blew me away!

Always smile, and be personal. As an interviewer, I want the person to feel passionate that this is the only job that matters to them. Be an active listener, and don't interrupt or talk over the interviewer.

Don't answer a question if you don't know the answer.

I see this almost every time I conduct an interview. Interviewers appreciate when you say, "That's a great question, and I'll find the answer and get back to you."

Possible Interview Questions

What's your claim to fame since you've been on this earth? I was Vice President / Market Manager for six stations in Oxnard/Ventura and Santa Barbara when I asked a woman that very question, and her response was, "I defeated Ken Jennings, who held the longest winning streak of any Jeopardy contestant."

Her name was Nancy Zerg, and it came down to the final Jeopardy answer.

The final Jeopardy category was Business and Industry.

The clue: Most of this firm's seventy thousand seasonal white-collar employees work only four months a year.

Correct response: H&R Block.

Jennings guessed FedEx, and Nancy Zerg guessed right and knocked off Jennings. He won over $2 million.

I didn't hire her, but that was the best response to that question I have ever heard!

What are your biggest strengths? Think of two or three strengths before you go into an interview so you will be ready for the answer.

What's your biggest weakness? I have many answers for this question, but my best answer is, "The fact that you haven't hired me yet."

You really need to think about what you need to work on without losing the job. Another fantastic answer if someone asks you what your biggest strengths would be, "My strengths greatly outweigh my weaknesses, but I believe you can always improve and innovate.

*These Next Interviewing Questions Are Designed
to See How You Answer Under Pressure*

Why should I hire you if there are tons of people applying for this position? What makes you stand out?

Tell me a tough situation you were in, and how did you get out of it? I have asked that question a lot!

Since I don't know you, what wouldn't I like in three months?

Tell me about a rude customer, and how did you handle it?

What's your biggest regret?

Who are your mentors, and why?

Tell me about a boss you loved and one you didn't care for, and why?

If you could change one thing about yourself, what would it be?

I remember I asked my daughter Demi if she could be anybody in this world, who would she like to be? Her answer was priceless.

She was about four years old, and she said, "I want to be Demi."

What can I say? She has great parents…LOL.

How would your friends describe you?

The final question you may be asked is, What do you want to leave me with before you walk out? This question was asked to me before I left an interview at Jacor Communications for my first general manager position in Denver, Colorado.

Frank Wood, the President of Jacor Communications, asked me, "What do you want to leave us with? I was almost out the door when he asked that question, so I slowly closed the door walked right up to his table put both hands on the table, looked him right in the eyes and said, "If we were at war right now, you would want me in the foxhole beside you."

I turned around and walked out the door. You guessed right, I got the job two weeks later!

Ask Your Potential Boss a Few Questions

You should always feel free to ask questions like the following:

What is your management style?

What type of person do you like on your team?
What do you look for in an outstanding employee?
Is there an opportunity for growth?
What do you personally like most about this company?

Asking your potential boss questions shows interest. Do a background check on your potential boss and company. That's what the Internet is for!

Post-Interview/Handwritten Thank-You Note

Shake hands, thank him or her for their time, go home, and write a handwritten thank-you note. Better yet, bring one with you, and write it out in the lobby, and leave it for the receptionist. People delete e-mails but save handwritten cards. Trust me, this makes you stand out!

Follow up two days later with a call if you haven't heard anything and once a week after that if you still haven't heard anything.

Writer's Block

If you ever have writer's block, say to yourself, "I'd like to tell you that…," and the next thing out of your mouth is the first sentence.

The first sentence should also grab their attention and make them want to read on. Here is an example:

Your company exceeds all my expectations!

Negotiating Your Salary

Never take the first offer! I don't care how excited you are. Show them that you need time to think about it. If the offer isn't what you want, say you were hoping the position offered a higher salary. If they don't want to budge on salary, ask for another week of vacation or a bonus if you overachieve expectations. Show them that you are a strong negotiator and will use that talent to benefit the company once they hire you!

I'd also have an attorney review the offer before you sign anything! Remember, scared money loses, so be confident, and always ask for the order!

Go Where You Are Wanted

You possibly will be faced with multiple job offers at one time, and my best advice is to go where you are wanted. Money, location, and title are important, but there is no better feeling than a company telling you we really want you here

Unfortunately, when you aren't being recognized or heard by your current boss and you decide to leave, they finally realize your worth. Sometimes you have to get an offer from another company to make the company you are working for see your value.

Never Search for a Job Without a Job but There Are Exceptions!

Overall, I agree with this strategy because you are coming from a position of strength with a job; however, one of the best jobs I ever got was when I was unemployed. I was working as, General Sales Manager at POWER 99 in Philadelphia, making a ton of money for my age, and everything was going great. The problem was, I thought my boss had a brilliant programming mind, but possessed horrible people skills.

We had a department head meeting in his office one morning, and he was berating our business manager in front of her husband, who was the chief engineer, and all the department heads. Everyone in the room was just cringing in their seats, wondering if they were going to be humiliated next. After the meeting, I stayed behind, closed the door, and sat down right in front of him. I looked him in the eye and told him if he ever spoke to my wife like he just did to our business manager (I wasn't married at the time) I would have beaten the shit out of him. I then resigned and said I couldn't work for a man like him. So I packed up my apartment and moved to the Jersey Shore.

NOW WHAT?

I had a house on 18th street in Ship Bottom, New Jersey, and had a bunch of friends coming to town for the Fourth of July weekend. I was up for two radio management jobs: General Sales Manager for WKQS in Chicago or General Manager for Jacor Communications in Denver. Remember, I'm currently unemployed! I already interviewed prior for both jobs after I resigned in Philadelphia, but the general manager in Chicago needed an answer by 3:00 p.m. on Thursday prior to the Fourth of July weekend in 1987.

That prior Monday, I called the President of Jacor, Frank Wood, and asked him if he was able to make a decision before 3:00 p.m. Thursday, and he said no. Now, I had to put my big-boy pants on and make a tough decision. I had five friends flying-in to the shore for the Fourth of July weekend, and they were all wondering what I was going to do at 3:00 p.m. Thursday.

My friend Tom Glazer was sitting with me waiting for 3:00 p.m. to roll around, and he said, "Well, Bobby, old boy, what are you going to do?"

At 3:00 p.m., I called the General Manager at WKQS, Mike Donovan, who was a great guy and friend and said, "If you need an answer at 3:00 p.m. and I have the chance to be a general manager at age thirty, the answer is no."

Mike thanked me and said I was out of the running now.

Around 3:10 p.m., my phone rang, and it was Frank Wood and the executives at Jacor Communications in Cincinnati, Ohio on a speakerphone. Frank said, "We were wondering what did you tell the guy from Chicago?"

I told Frank, "If I have an opportunity to be a General Manager for Jacor Communications, then I'll risk losing the job in Chicago."

Frank paused for a second and then said, "Good, because we want to hire you!"

I was so excited I couldn't stand it. I thanked them all, and the lesson here is, *sometimes, you have to take huge risks that can be life-changing, and that one was mine.* My friends and I partied like rock stars that weekend!

Watch professional poker players play Texas Hold 'em, and see how they go all-in with nothing in their hand. They sense weakness from the other player or players and act on it. You have to read the room and go with your gut instincts because your gut is always right.

Save 10% of Every Check and Possibly Retire in Your Forties

Put your money in a mutual fund or 401(k), and never touch it! It will compound and grow every year, and when you check it once per year, you'll have a huge smile on your face. Don't buy individual stocks if you aren't an expert. Also, hire a financial planner, and stick to the plan he or she lays out.

One of the best weekends of my life

Around my fortieth birthday, my French friend, Pascal Stolz, invited me to play golf in Monterey, California. I had no idea what courses we were going to play, but I was always up for golf. I was totally shocked because it was three weeks before my fortieth birthday and he was working for Cobra Golf when he told me they were having an event he wanted me to go to.

We woke up in a cheap hotel, and he told me that we were playing Cypress Point at 7:30 a.m. I was so excited I couldn't stand it. We were the guests of Gary Vandeweghe, an attorney for Cobra Golf. Gary was the youngest member ever to become a member of Cypress Point and an amazing man. He was the person I asked if I had a lot of money where should I invest it? He told me mutual funds, and I listened to his advice.

I shot seventy-six that day, at Cypress Point, and pared the sixteenth par-3 hole over the water into the wind. Oddly enough, three weeks later, Gary and I were in Hawaii the same week and played golf a few more times together with his amazing family.

After we played Cypress Point, Pascal told me we weren't done, and we were teeing off at Pebble Beach at 1:30 p.m. and shot eighty-six. I told Pascal I was physically and mentally drained, in a good way and wanted to go take a shower and rest up at the hotel. Pascal said we really have to make an appearance at the Cobra Golf Event, so I reluctantly joined him. We walked into the Lodge at Pebble Beach, and at the end of the hall, in one of the banquet rooms, sixty-five of my family and closest friends from all over the country surprised me for my fortieth birthday. It was probably one of the greatest, most memorable weekends of my life besides the births of my three children! My wife at the time had one more surprise for me and escorted me to the balcony at Pebble Beach overlooking the 18th hole. It was Sal Spoto, my best friend since we were five years old. Sal and I both broke down in tears and hugged it out. We both came from nothing, and now I was able to treat him to play our dream course together on my fortieth birthday. Dreams do come true! The lesson here is, *sometimes you will be reluctant to try new things or pass up invitations, but you never know what surprises will lurk.*

Manage Your Addiction to Technology / Smartphones / Video Games / Laptops / Tobacco and Alcohol

I'm not saying that technology is bad. I just think most of us are addicted to technology, and that is a bad thing. There is an app called Moment, which tracks how much time a day you spend on your phone. If you get it and use it, you'll be shocked at the results! If you text and drive, it's just a matter of time before you cause an accident, kill someone, or kill yourself. You are just not that damn important, nor is anyone else that can't wait a few minutes until you pull off the road and call when you get to your destination. We are losing that personal face-to-face interaction that is so necessary.

I say to people that have lost a loved one, "If you had one minute to have them back, would you want to text them or speak to them in person?"

Put your cell phone in your car's glove box, and take it out when you arrive at your destination. It may save your or someone else's life. Also, shut your phone off at night so you can sleep. Don't ever bring your phone into an interview…period! I have interviewed people that didn't silence their phones; took them out; put them on the table; or in one case, actually took the call. Needless to say, none of those people were hired.

Next time you go to a restaurant, take a good look around and see all the people on their cell phones. I watched a family where the mom and dad were busy texting on their cell phones, while their kids were playing video games on their iPads. No words were spoken, and I should have said something! This is a communication breakdown that needs to be addressed.

If you go to dinner with friends and you place your iPhone on the table, you are basically saying I cannot give you all my attention, and it's extremely rude. There is a place for smartphones but know it is an addiction, and you need to harness it at times.

You Are Always Being Monitored

You are being watched 24-7 so choose your words and actions wisely. Don't post drunk or stoned photos, bragging about your new tattoos, etc., on any of the social media sites. Employers watch what you post and do background and drug tests, so don't lose the job before you apply. I recently had a guy pitch me for a job that was outstanding until I did a background check and drug test. The background check showed he was previously in jail for stealing a car and had THC in his bloodstream. Sometimes you can't judge a book by its cover.

My youngest daughter, Sophia, was applying for an internship at a major broadcast company, and her boss, who is a friend, told me to have her take down some of her drinking photos from college on Instagram. You are always being watched, and that is a great way not to get an interview or to lose your dream job.

Don't Be Afraid to Ask for What You Want

Most people are afraid to ask for the order. My boss, Marc Morgan, at WPLJ radio in New York City taught me a very important lesson on getting what you didn't think wasn't possible. There was a guy who handled many rock clubs on Long Island, and he spent a lot of money with my radio station. Every year, we would take him out to an all-afternoon lunch, eat and drink way too much, and then negotiate a rate for the next year. My boss would come for lunch and leave the negotiation up to me. Our goal was to get his rate up from $150 per spot to $165.

To make a long story short, I came back to my boss with a $160 rate, and he said he wasn't going to accept that rate. He needed $165. I was beyond pissed but got on the phone, called my client, and told him we needed $185 per spot, or we would have to walk. I waited in silence for about twenty seconds, which seemed like an eternity. He said he wasn't happy with the rate increase but agreed to pay it.

I later walked into my boss's office, and he asked, "Did you get $165?"

I told him no and threw the order on his desk at $185 per spot. *If you don't ask, you won't get it, never be afraid to ask for the order with confidence!*

There will be many times in your life when you think you know the outcome before it happens. My advice is, *never assume anything*.

Take a Bad Situation and Turn It into a Good One

In 2003, I lost my job as market manager for six top radio stations in Los Angeles in a merger which is now called iHeartRadio. We moved the family down to San Diego, and I started selling real estate for Willis Allen in Del Mar, California. This next story is a great lesson.

A lady in my neighborhood had a for-sale-by-owner sign on her front lawn called an FSBO in Encinitas Ranch, California. I rang her doorbell and told her the advantages of using a licensed Realtor. I explained I could market the property, negotiate a fair price, and since I live in the development, I know everything positive about living there. She told me to come back Friday, and when I came to her door, she clearly had the flu. I told her I was going away on a ski trip over the weekend and could she just sign the contract. She told me not to worry and come back on Monday.

When I came home from my ski trip, I was so excited to possibly get my first listing. I rang the doorbell, and she greeted me by saying, "Oh Bob, I'm sorry. I panicked over the weekend and listed with another agent."

I was so upset but kept my temper and told her, "I prepared a Comparative Market Analysis (CMA) for your property that took me a few hours, and since Realtors only have their time, please don't do what you did to me to the next agent."

Two days later I drove past her house to see what agent she listed her home with? In February it gets dark at 5 p.m. and I drove by her home approximately 6:30 p.m. and couldn't barely see there was a sign posted. I came up with an idea to light up the signs and change the real estate industry as we know it!

We sold twenty thousand Listinglights in seven countries, but the crash of 2008 not only killed the real estate industry. It basically cost me everything! We lost our homes. The stock market crash took our cash and retirement funds, and it was the toughest time of my life. I have a wife and three kids and no money. Credit card companies were charging outrageous interest rates and felt the walls closing in on me! I said enough is enough and got back into radio, which is my wheelhouse and commuted on weekends, 166 miles from San Diego to Ventura County because I promised my kids I wouldn't move them once they attended high school.

The lesson here is giving up is easy, but working through the tough times is what builds character. I was sure that when the money was gone, it was going to hurt or kill my marriage, and I was right. I was divorced in 2012.

My X-wife gave me three amazing children and a famous quote which is, "If attitudes are contagious…" is yours worth catching?

Forgiveness Gene!

If I struggle with anything in my life, it's the forgiveness gene! I know that you should forgive people and give them a second chance, but I was always very loyal to family, friends, employers, and coworkers. When someone violates my trust, I struggle to get over it. So I promise, I am working on this, but *you* should always forgive and give a second chance, especially if the person shows remorse. I was told that when you forgive, you are releasing yourself, not them. By not giving forgiveness, you are carrying that weight around, and it's wasted energy! Social media is full of a lot of negative posts and you can't please everyone so don't try. There was one guy that hated me in the Fraternity, and it bothered the shit out of me. I went to the president of Phi Kappa Psi at the time, Bob Byrd and asked him what I should do to turn this guy around. He gave me advice that I now live by. He said there are 107 brothers in the fraternity, 106 love you, yet you give all your energy to the one that doesn't? Let the haters hate but just focus and surround yourself with positive people.

Have Self-Confidence

I've met tons of really creative people that lack self-confidence. They are always looking for reassurance and acceptance. You have to believe in yourself and know from the inside out you are special. Everyone has special talents, but only you know what your insides are capable of. So my advice is, *confidence is attractive to employers, so be confident, not cocky*. Take "I" and "me" out of your vocabulary as much as possible, and replace it with our, we, and us.

Jordan Spieth was the first professional golfer to acknowledge that he cannot achieve the success he has without his team. Golf isn't an individual sport at the professional level, so good job, Jordan, for recognizing you didn't do it alone!

Recognize Big Chances to Make Huge Money

I still suffer over this one, but here it goes. I was working in a Silicon Valley for a startup in Mountain View, California called Sonicbox. It was an Internet Radio Network, and we were way ahead of our time. I was commuting two times a week from Los Angeles, and on a cab ride home, I bought one thousand shares of Apple at $11 a share. This is back in 1999. I sold it at $18 and thought I was a genius. Well, I don't want to do the math, but let's say I would be worth millions if I kept it.

These deals do happen in one's lifetime, but the key is to trust your gut and go for it. You can make more mistakes at a young age than when you are older, so take some risks, and live your life. Bitcoin went up 2000 percent in the first few months! I still recommend hiring a professional for anything you aren't.

Persistence

The meaning of persistence is firm continuance in a course of action in spite of difficulty or opposition. The key words here are difficulty or opposition. People like when you are persistent as long as it isn't stalking persistence or annoying persistence. There is a line so get close to it, but don't go over it.

Being Cheap Is a Major Turn Off

Everyone hates a cheap person, and we all know a few! I can't think of a bigger turnoff than someone not paying his or her fair share when the bill comes. My former father-in-law always laughed at guys trying to go for their wallets, with no intent of actually picking up the tab! I have met many people like that, and it isn't attractive.

People that only care about money don't understand that money isn't everything. Money is freedom, but you should live each day to its fullest. How many people do you know that saved up for a lifetime, retired, and dropped dead? See what I mean? Enjoy every minute on this great earth because you never know when it's going to end! Also, people that just chase money are not focusing on the right thing. If you work hard and try to be the best at whatever you do, the money will follow.

Every job I ever had, I tried to be the best and was very competitive. No wasn't in my vocabulary! I worked harder, smarter, and had more energy than my coworkers. Employers took notice, and I became a general manager at a major radio station in Denver at age thirty. The money kept coming, but that wasn't the driving force.

NOW WHAT?

Don't Drink and Drive

Thank God for Uber and Lyft. A DUI probably costs you upward of $10,000 in legal fees and goes on your record for life. An Uber or Lyft trip, in most instances, is less than $25. If you do the math, it makes a ton of sense. Always have a designated driver if your group plans on drinking or hire a driver.

Texting and Driving Makes a Horrible Mix

It amazes me that people can focus on driving a weapon while texting and driving. Most car accidents occur in a split second, and that's all it takes to look at your phone, never mind texting! How many people need to die before you get this through your heads, either pull over or wait until you get to your destination. Let me say it again, "You are not that damn important than a text, finding the right song on the radio or phone call can't wait until you arrive." If you want to stay alive don't text and drive.

Never Drink in Excess at Company Functions

There are many horror stories about this one, but one really stands out. I was working at WPLJ in New York City, and our boss took us out for drinks after work. One of our salespeople got a bit tipsy and let him know how she felt about him. Needless to say, she was cleaning her desk out the next day. One or two drinks are tolerable, but never get intoxicated! Remember to eat and drink one glass of water for every drink you have. The need to get blacked out drunk was a concept I never understood. The average person gets drunk on three to five drinks, so why the need to have ten to fifteen drinks?

Remember People's Names

Don't ever say, "I can't remember a person's name!" A person's name is sacred to them, so the rules are correctly pronounce their name and then say their name a few times while shaking their hand. I'll also write a handwritten note for almost everyone I meet in person if we can beneficially help one another. How many times do you see someone for the second time and forget his or her name? Now, on the other hand, if you remember their name, what type of impact will that make? One more tip, make sure you spell it correctly.

I misspelled the name of a major media buyer in Los Angeles on the first page of my presentation, and the rest of my pitch fell on deaf ears. Needless to say, I never made that mistake again. Always check and recheck the spelling of names of people you are presenting to.

Networking Is a Must / Social Media

My brother, Rich, is an attorney in Southern New Jersey, and I have told him for years to network with people that can help his business. That fell on deaf ears for years, but what do you know? In the past five to ten years, he is now listening, and he has more business than he can handle. He goes to bars, restaurants, charity events and has happy hour for real estate agents, etc. Networking is vital, and one person can lead to many more. Social media is also a necessity nowadays. If you don't know how to do it, hire an expert and make sure your business is on Snapchat, LinkedIn, Facebook, Instagram, and any industry websites that can help move your business forward.

Social media can also hurt your business by posting your political views or personal opinions! Remember, not everyone thinks like you do, so it's best to keep your opinions and views away from potential new customers.

Hire Positive Attitudes and Never Surround Yourself with Mediocrity

A former Southwest Airlines CEO, Herb Kelleher, had a TV commercial years ago where he said Southwest only hires positive attitudes and boy, was he right. When I lived in Dallas and worked at KISS-FM, I always traveled on Southwest Airlines, and the crew was always positive and fun.

NOW WHAT?

Attitude is the first thing I look for when I'm interviewing someone. I know in five minutes if I'm going to hire someone, and it's because of my positive attitude radar…LOL. Negativity in an organization is a cancer that needs to be eradicated immediately! A bad attitude kills morale, and it turns everyone around them in a negative way. I was always sent to troubled radio stations and was called, "The Hatchet Man," "Killer V," "V Sting," and other words probably not appropriate for print. The bottom line was eliminating the negative people and surrounding myself with loyal positive people that made shit happen! Every station I worked at was in better shape at my departure than upon my arrival.

Rate Your Staff

If you are in charge of a staff and I asked you to give me a number one to ten, how would you rate your staff? If it is below seven, then start replacing the people that are bringing the rest of the team down. One of my rules on hiring someone was, "Can I eat dinner with this person?" If the answer was no then I didn't hire them!

Don't Ever Say That's Not My Job to Your Boss

If you want to get ahead in the corporate world, you should volunteer for everything that can help you. I have been a senior-level manager for over thirty years and when someone tells me that's not their job, I immediately feel different about that person. It shows me they aren't a team player or they possibly will be a problem moving forward. I don't mean to do anything unethical; I'm saying if it will help the team, volunteer.

Recently, I had an employee tell me she didn't want to do a job we needed her to do. I told her that is the job, and if you don't like it, I will find someone who does! Saying you don't want to do something your boss needs to be done is just as bad as telling your boss that's not my job, so don't do either.

Most People Are Followers, so if You Want to Stand Out, Be a Leader

It amazes me how true this is!

People are sheep, which means they need someone or something to follow. If a celebrity endorses a product, the sheep will buy it. So if you want to stand out, be a leader and let people follow you. I don't understand why you need someone to tell you how to feel, what not to do or buy, or anything else. You are an adult, so make adult decisions on your own. You aren't always going to be right, but a bad decision is better than not making one at all. You can always correct a bad decision; just don't prolong how long you want it to be bad. I read *The Richest Man in Babylon*, and the moral of the story is to get other people to work for you!

Always Be on Time/No Sacred Cows

Arrive five minutes early, and never one minute late. You hear people saying they can never be on time. Well, I don't buy it. When you are late, you are disrespecting the person running the meeting and the people in the meeting that are waiting for you.

I was hired as General Manager of a major radio station in San Francisco, KYLD/WILD 107, now called WILD 94.9. The owners flew in from the East Coast and met me in our San Francisco office before we would go and announce my appointment to the staff. The owners told me there was one sacred cow. Meaning, don't fire this person and to be nice. I'll not mention his name, but here's what happened. It's 9:00 a.m., and I like to start my meetings on time. The owners asked me to give the program director a few extra minutes, and I reluctantly agreed. After ten minutes I said to the owners, "I'm not waiting for a prima donna, so let's go," and they followed me in the conference room with about fifty staffers.

About twenty minutes after the meeting started, the program director waltzes in, and in front of everyone, I said to him, "Since you like personal attention, wait for me in my office, and I'll give you all the personal attention you need after the meeting."

When you are the leader, you need to set the tone with your employees. I'm sure my bosses were shitting their pants, but after the meeting, we walked into my office, and the program director was waiting. I looked him right in the eyes and said, "If you ever come late to another one of my meetings again, I'll fire you!'

I then asked him if I was clear, and he said, "Yes."

The owners were in shock. I fired this person three weeks later, and in eighteen months we beat the number one hip-hop station in the market. I don't believe in sacred cows, just team players. If you want to stand out, that's fine, but don't disrespect the team or me.

One of my mentors, John Hare, whom I worked for in KISS in Dallas told me, "When you first start a senior level management job, set the tone, and let them know what you expect from them and what they can expect from you."

I think a clear message was sent that day!

Accept Responsibility No Matter How Difficult It Is

Most people can tell when a person is lying, so don't make excuses. I probably hate excuses more than anything. People who play the blame game infuriates me! When a company makes mistakes and admits it, we all move on. If a company or person hides the truth and it comes out later, they are marked forever, just ask President Clinton. If President Clinton had admitted his mistake and took responsibility, we would have healed a lot sooner, and a lot more time would have been spent on running the country instead of covering up the truth.

We all make mistakes, and as I always say, **a mistake is when an error repeats itself**, but we still do. When you do make a mistake, admit it, and make the proper apologies. You won't be able to sleep at night if you keep it in, and we've all been there. The truth will set you free! Gary Hart probably could have been one of the best Presidents this country would have ever seen, but one mistake with Donna Rice cost him his political future. A lot of you younger readers may have no idea what I'm talking about so just Google it… LOL. Gary Hart was the first casualty of a sex scandal, and derailed his front runner position for President of the United States in 1984.

Funny coincidence is that Gary Hart and I were members of the Denver Athletic Club and his locker was right next to mine. Thank God I didn't go on that fishing trip…LOL.

The truth always comes out, so just know, you are only getting away with something for a period of time. In that time, guilt will kill your insides, give you sleepless nights, etc. We all make mistakes, and when you admit them, it will blow over a lot sooner.

This is a bad story, but sometimes, the truth will set you free. One night, a bunch of my fraternity brothers and I went to Pittsburgh to get some turf from the Pitt Panthers football field. Stupid idea? It was a few weeks before Christmas and the middle of winter in Pittsburgh. The ground was so frozen we couldn't get a shovel into the ground to go under the fence, so we drove home from Pittsburgh and arrived in Morgantown around 2:00 a.m.

The night wasn't a total waste because we needed to get a Christmas tree for our fraternity house. We drove in some upscale neighborhoods and saw this beautiful tree on the front lawn of this really nice house. My roommate and pledge brother, Jeff Carmichael, and I went under the tree with a finger saw and chopped it down. At about 3:00 a.m., we got pulled over by the WVU security police, and they asked us where we got the tree. To make a long story short, we took them to the home of the people we stole the tree from and rang their doorbell at approximately 3:30 a.m. A lady answered the door in her robe and asked what the problem was. I confessed to chopping the tree down for the fraternity house on their front lawn, and her husband joined in and asked what fraternity. I told him Phi Kappa Psi, and he said he was a brother and gave me the secret handshake. He said he wasn't going to press charges and said to put a sign up that he donated the tree. He went on to say if we needed a tree next year, there are plenty in his backyard.

Well, you think that was the end of it but boy, were we wrong! The next day, we found out that the tree we stole was one of the active fraternity member's girlfriend's house. Since he was a regular member, called an active, and we were pledges, let's just say we did push-ups and sit-ups in the mud on the fraternity house's front lawn until we dropped. Jeff and I always joked that one of us wouldn't make it to age 30 and unfortunately Jeff was killed tragically in a car accident a few months later. RIP my friend...

My son, Johnny, was on the high school football team at La Costa Canyon, and a bunch of his football buddies were drinking in a bus across from school, and he got caught. My son was not a starter, so the next day, he was called in by the principal and head coach, and Johnny admitted to drinking while the starting players didn't own up to it. Johnny was severely punished by being suspended, going to alcohol classes, and being kicked off the football team. Johnny took the fall for his alleged brothers on the football team, and I am still hot over this situation. Where I come from, the entire team would have accepted blame, but they left Johnny out to dry.

The next day, I went crazy and demanded to speak to the principal and whoever made the decision to suspend my son while the others got off scot-free. Well, they gave me a bunch of bullshit and made an example out of my son. I sent an email to his football coach and started off by saying, "I'd call you coach if you deserved the title." If Johnny was kicked off the team, all the other players should have had the same fate, but even at the high school level, there is massive politics.

All the starting players had a game next week and lost 45/0 and boy was karma a bitch. I'm proud of my son, and that is how we taught him. No matter how bad you mess up, accept the consequences, and move forward. Johnny's teammates will have to live with what they did. Moreover, the coach probably will never give it a second thought.

How Can You Make a Difference If You Do What Everybody Else Is Doing!

I wish more companies understood this!

You have to hire people that are creative and challenge policy. Just because a company has a policy, doesn't mean it is right. I was called "The Man You Love to Hate" because I was different and took creative risks. My competitors hated me, and my staffs loved me. I was a leader, not a manager and always listened to new creative, cutting edge ideas.

In Denver, at 103.5 THE FOX radio station, we gave away the first breast augmentation and advertised our new morning show, Dave Rickards and Abby Bonnel, on six of our competitors' radio stations, after we hired an advertising agency in Tampa, Florida, to come up with a jingle for *Morning Flakes*, which was the name of our new morning show. Our competitors thought it was a cereal and didn't catch the mistake for three days! In Chicago, at WLS/FM, we came up with "Sing Yourself to Hawaii" with Steve Dahl and Garry Meier and sold a sponsorship to American Airlines.

We would plan periodic morning show suspensions for the Dog House on WILD 94.9 to create a buzz and fire up the listeners. We launched the largest bumper sticker campaign in Chicago at WLS with Pepsi and had three million bumper stickers all over town and distributed them at Dominick's food store locations all over Chicagoland. These are things that made us stand out.

In West Virginia, we had a promotion called, "Name the Seven Wonders of West Virginia."

If we just follow policy, how can anyone stand out?

Don't Ignore Life's Wake-Up Calls

I always trust my gut instincts and you should too. Once you make a decision, don't second-guess yourself. You can always fix a bad decision, and it's better to make a bad decision than not make one at all. An indecisive leader lacks followers!

Family first is also something we take for granted at times. Your job isn't more important than your family. If you work for a boss that doesn't understand that, look for one that does!

Your health is extremely important as well, and your body doesn't lie. If something is bothering you, go to the doctor immediately. I worked at the Garfield, New Jersey, Volunteer Ambulance Corps for five years and have seen many people not take care of themselves and have to be rushed to the ER.

NOW WHAT?

My son Johnny and I pitched the Listinglight with Billy Mays and Anthony Sullivan

Me, my mom, Lois, Sal's mom, Marilyn and Sal

My son proud to wear the Visotcky name in
Pop Warner Encinitas, California

My brother Rich and I at my Dad's Mayor Memorial Ceremony

NOW WHAT?

Graduation from Kindergarten at Our Lady of Sorrows in Garfield, N.J.

Me and my best friend Sal Spoto at Nardi's at the Jersey shore

BOB VISOTCKY

My 450sl Mercedes and house in Evergreen at age 30

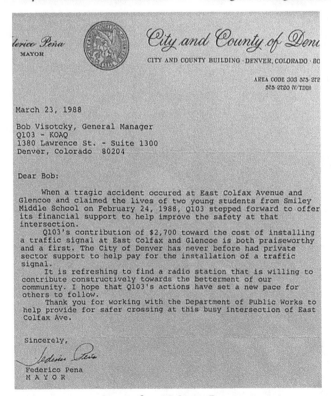

Letter from Mayor Pena

NOW WHAT?

My photo at the Palm in Los Angeles

Dancing with my kids at a wedding in Lake Tahoe

My son wanted a family picture post divorce Christmas 2018

Made the cover of FMQB when I was Los Angeles VP/Market Manager

NOW WHAT?

All the Denver GM's on the cover of
Advertising&Marketing Review

 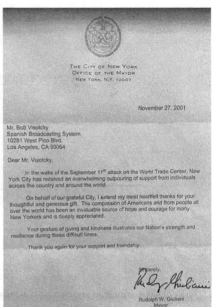

Sent the Mayor a poster of the Twin Towers with two American flags draped over them and he sent me this letter.

My office bulletin board with photos of my radio memories

NOW WHAT?

My Listinglight invention at work!

This photo actually won a photo contest when I was 5 years old

I was the lead in every play in grammar
School from Kindergarten on

My brother Rich and I in the Garfield
Volunteer Ambulance Corps.

NOW WHAT?

My grandpa John and grandma Edee

Roasted my dad at his retirement party from
Public Service Electric and Gas

Member of Phi Kappa Psi at West Virginia University

Playing at a WPLJ softball charity event against the Mamas and the Papas team called THE ABUSERS!

If you have something good going on in your life, don't ever take it for granted. You have to stop and smell the roses sometimes and appreciate the outstanding life you are leading!

Share What You Learn (Pay It Forward)

I gave a speech at a broadcasting class at Palomar College in San Diego for my friend, Professor Dean Goss. My topic was "How to Prepare for the Real World." I guess it should have been called "Now What." LOL. I introduced myself, gave a quick bio, and then got into the meat of my speech. The professor, Dean Goss, told me there was a kid in the back of the class that just listens to music on his headphones with his open laptop and never interacts with others. I just looked at Dean and smiled. During my speech, I interviewed some students and asked the tough questions. A young lady went first and told me she wanted to be an actress, and after about five questions, I told her I wouldn't have hired her. She was taken aback and asked why? I told her I didn't feel it and where is the passion?

Later in the class, I had some students come up and give the class a three-minute speech on what they are passionate about. The girl that wanted to be an actress that I spoke of earlier asked if she could go first, and I said sure. She got up and did a one-act play that had everyone give her standing ovation at the conclusion. I swear the hair on my arms was raised, and I was never so impressed. She took a positive critique and excelled way beyond anyone in that classroom's expectations. (*Listen to constructive criticism.*)

Then the unexpected occurred, remember the student that never interacts with others, keeps his headphones, and laptop up all the time? Well, he raised his hand, removed his headphones, and asked if he could move to the front of the classroom and say a few words. I welcomed him up front, and the students were mesmerized. He stood up in front of the class and said that he has never felt this comfortable in a public setting before and that he loved everyone in the class. Dean, his professor, came up to me, a few inches from my face, and showed a tear coming down his face.

That's passion baby and further inspired me to write this book. Go on a speaking tour, and tell people to believe in themselves, get the proper guidance, and never give up. People want and need inspirational leadership, so if you are going to be a leader, not manager, inspire people!

When Asked to Speak in Front of a Crowd, Are You Excited or Scared?

If you are prepared, you are excited. If you are not prepared, you are nervous. Practice in front of a mirror, or ask someone to video your practice speech. People remember three things: Coke Is It, appreciate the moment, believe in yourself, change is good, etc. Most speakers go too long and like to hear themselves talk. Give your audience three key facts that they can use and remember, and you will be known before you are needed. It's important to have a strong entrance and exit when speaking to a crowd or selling anything. Professional athletes still have their heart rate race and palms get sweaty before they compete. The difference is they trained their bodies that these feelings are caused by excitement, not fear. The saying "Never let them see you sweat" never applied to "Mean Joe Green" from the Pittsburgh Steelers!

Quitting Is the Easy Way Out

Take can't out of your vocabulary. The guitar was so hard to learn, but I stuck with it, practiced until my fingers calloused up, and got decent but not great. I love anyone that can play an instrument or sing. Music is so powerful and in a lot of cases, a mood setter. Everyone hates a quitter and loves a winner. Be a winner! My grandfather was big on if you are going to start something…finish it! Instead of saying I can't, say I'm having difficulty right now, but I'll get it!

Be a Difference Maker

I probably have never followed many rules because the status quo bores me, and I hate authority. My dad was really tough on me, so I think if I were meeting with a shrink, he'd probably say that had a lot to do with it! If everybody's doing everything the same way, how can you ever make a difference or stand out? Difference makers don't always follow structure. They let their creativity take them wherever it wanted to go.

Difference makers anticipate changes and trends in the market before they happen. Most companies are so afraid of lawsuits now that they have lost their creative edge! If your staff thinks that they won't get fired, they will take advantage of every possible situation: call in sick more, leave early, etc. You need to take charge of the situation before the inmates run the asylum.

More on Mentors

I was fortunate to work with some of the best people in the business and learned what and not to do. Some of my mentors are Larry Divney, Marty Greenberg, John Hare, Jimmy de Castro, Dale Miller, Nick Trigony, Joe Parish, Frank Wood, Don Bouloukos, Marc Morgan, Allen Shaw, Bobby Lawrence, and Randy Michaels to name a few. I met Terry Hardin, an intern at KISS 106 in Dallas. He was a student at SMU, and I asked him what he wanted to do after graduation.

He replied, "Go to San Diego and surf."

I laughed and explained that I see a lot of talent in him and can make him a successful radio executive. Terry worked for me in sales in Philadelphia, then sales at 103.5 The Fox in Denver, and general sales manager at MIX 94.9/San Diego. We split up in Cleveland when he was my general sales manager at WMJI due to a sale, and Terry became a general manager in Chicago and later director of sales for Emmis Communications over the entire company. I think one of the best compliments I ever received was from the former CEO of Evergreen Media, Scott Ginsburg. Scott told people attending a radio convention in Phoenix that after Jimmy de Castro, I was the next guy he would send in to fix a radio station. Jimmy de Castro is the best boss I ever worked for because he let me be me. I worked for Jimmy de Castro at KYLD/San Francisco. MEGA 100 in Los Angeles named me the first market manager in the company, overseeing six stations in Denver, and then the ultimate job—market manager of Los Angeles—overseeing six top radio stations, 600 employees and $250-million in revenue.

Life was good until a huge curveball hit me. I was fired in Los Angeles due to a merger with Clear Channel, now called iHeartMedia. That was one of the lowest points of my life, but we are judged on how we handle adversity, and I needed to show my three children it's not the end of the world, just a new chapter. The lesson here is when one door closes, another one opens, or **a bouncing ball hits bottom before it bounces back**! The bouncing ball analogy really helped me!

The 2008 real-estate-market crash was our equivalent to the "Great Depression." Lenders were lending whatever they needed to close a loan, prior to the crash. People overextended themselves, and short sales and foreclosures were running rampant. I was always taught that if you want to own your own business, try and use other people's money such as banks and investors. You may not own 100% that way, but 50%, 60%, or 70% is better than zero! I made that cardinal mistake because I was so sure that my invention, the Listinglight, was a winner that I didn't anticipate a market crash in 2008. I lost everything! My houses, my business, and my wife were all casualties of the crash. This was the toughest time in my life, and I am stronger for that experience. Quitting would have been easy, but that was never an option. I went back into radio and slowly built my way back. **The lesson here is if you are going to start a new business, use other people's money and plan for the worst but hope for the best!**

Even though we lost a lot, my son, Johnny, said he was so proud of me for going all-in. That was all I needed to hear. That experience made me a stronger person and a better father, and it gave me a never-quit attitude.

NOW WHAT?

Four Keys to Build Your Brand

- Reach—Your goal is to get as many people as you can know you, via networking, social media, influencers, e-mail blasts, door-to-door, radio, TV, and print. Whatever it takes!
- Frequency—You have to reach someone today eight to twelve times before they get your attention, so my advice is to start small and work your way up.
- Consistency—To me, this is very important and where most fall short. You need to be consistently in front of the people you want to attract. Social media, blogs etc. The key is to be known before you are needed. Be an expert in your field and show value.
- Message—All your marketing materials should leave you with three key points to remember about you or your business. It's a fact that people are great at remembering things in threes. Just think how these phrases stayed in our brains, Coke is It, The Pepsi Generation, Stronger Than Dirt, Just Do It, etc. What are the three bullet points about you that tell me why someone should hire you?

So if you want to build your own brand, follow the four keys of branding!

Think Like an Owner

I know many salespeople and managers that have abused time off, expenses, giving away free stuff, etc. If they thought like an owner, they would never have done those things. It comes down to needs and wants. I want to buy my client a really expensive bottle of wine (thinking like a salesperson), but a less expensive bottle would do the same good (thinking like an owner). Every business I'm hired to turn around, I always think like an owner. If I'm selling commercials to a business, I put myself in his or her shoes and ask myself would buy this if I were the owner.

Be Known Before You Are Needed

If I asked you to name a Realtor, lawyer, plumber or carpet company, what comes to mind? The businesses that are consistent marketers have catchy jingles or have excellent locations. The first question I ask a business owner is, "Are you known before you are needed?" and "Do you have top of mind awareness with your customers?"

I walked into an attorney's office, and he basically blew me off and said he didn't need advertising because everyone knows him. The next week, I stood in front of his office where his sign was prominent with my recorder and asked people if they needed a lawyer whom would they recommend? Not one person mentioned the attorney whose sign we stood in front of. I went back into his office and told him the question I asked people and played it for him.

He stopped me after a few minutes of listening and said, "What mall did you do this at?"

I said, "I was standing right in front of your office!"

Let's just say he became a good customer for a long time.

I was also told many times that they don't need to advertise. They have more clients than they know what to do with, and everyone knows them.

I just looked at them and said, "Coke and McDonald's don't need to advertise, but they don't take their customers for granted."

Boom!

When you get a job, make sure your boss notices you being on time, having a positive attitude, willing to help others, etc. If you want to move up the ladder faster, be known before you are needed.

Look for the Positives in People Before the Negatives

People tend to search for what's wrong with a person before they find out what's right about a person, and that drives me crazy. If you start with what's right, you'd be surprised that you will find a lot more positive attributes than negative ones. We tend to prejudge people all the time, and that is so unfair. George Bush 43 at his dad's funeral said his dad always looked for the good in a person and always found it. Let's all learn from Bush 41.

Be a Good Listener

Being a good listener is a talent! You learn as you listen. You stagnate when you talk. Don't interrupt a person in midsentence. I love watching interviewers on TV that are more interested in what questions they are asking instead of listening to the answer to the question they just asked. If someone gives an opinion that you totally disagree with, start by saying I see your point or understand why you feel that way, then make your point. Most people want to be heard, so listen.

Never Answer a Question If You Don't Know the Answer

We all hate a know-it-all, so if you don't know the answer to a question, don't fake it. It's much better to say that is an excellent question and let me find out the answer. With Google at your fingertips, a lot of answers can be easily found. Sometimes I'll ask a question I already know the answer to see how the person I'm interviewing responds.

Read Five Hours a Week (One Hour Per Day)

Most successful people read and learn. If you set one hour a day and read self-help books, you'll get out of your comfort zone, and new ideas will blossom. Books such as *Who Moved My Cheese, One Minute Manager, Ninja Selling,* and *Dress for Success* were very helpful in my career development. Biographies of interesting people were also of great interest to me and still are. Never stop learning and asking questions.

Don't Cheat in Golf or in Anything for that Matter

I can tell a lot about a person in one round of golf! If they move their ball out of a hazard, I know they don't mind cheating. If they lose their temper or throw a club, I know they don't have a lot of self-control. If they tell you they had a four and not a six, they can't be trusted. If they mark the ball two inches closer and think nobody saw it, they are only cheating themselves. If they dress sloppily, it shows disrespect. If they walk in your line, they have no regard for others. If they show disrespect to caddies, they are a narcissus. I think by now you get the idea! At the end of the round, you should take your hat off, look the players in their eyes, shake their hands, and tell them how much fun you had that day.

Player or Victim

In a book called *Ninja Selling* by Larry Kendall, they discuss two types of sellers: the player or the victim. The player sends off a positive vibe, has lots of energy, is well informed, and is the entire package. The victim has negative energy and looks at what's bad first than what's good. This person is wo-wo-is-me. People gravitate to players, not victims!

They also discuss how your brain expands on what you are focusing on. If a golfer sees water on the left side and focuses on it, that's where the ball is going. A professional golfer focuses on the fairway, and the water doesn't come into focus. Focus on positive outcomes than negative outcomes, and you'll be much happier and successful.

Time Healer

We probably all have lost someone special in our lives or had a good friend move away, etc. The hurt is unbearable at the onset, but time has a way to make things better and clearer. Losing a loved one is the worst, but I think they would like you to move on and remember the good times you shared. I heard that life is meant for the living, so we have to keep moving forward.

I saw a quote on TV that said, "Life can only be understood backward, but it must be lived forward."

Since history has a way of repeating itself, it's good to draw from the past but live for the future. Make every day count, and take nothing for granted.

Why Are We More Popular When We Are Dead?

Have you ever noticed that we idolize people when they are dead but did not appreciate them fully when they were still alive? President George Bush 41 was berated by the media when he was President and at the day of his passing, labeled one of the best one-term Presidents we ever had. The media always looks for what's wrong with a person when they are alive and then thinks it's okay to hail them in death. What hypocrisy! My advice to the youth is, spend more time with family members and learn about their life. You'd be amazed by how much wisdom your parents and friends have. You just need hang time and ask questions.

People Buy Anything for Two Reasons

It either solves a need, or it gives you pleasure. You need a new suit or dress for a party that gives you both! Think about your last purchase. What did you get out of it? This goes with needs and wants. If you are on a tight budget, buy what you need, not what you want.

Stand Up for Those Who Can't Stand Up for Themselves!

I hate bullies!

I have always stood up for people that were being threatened by someone more powerful, but I'll never forget what happened at Paramus Catholic Boys High School one glorious afternoon at Paramus Public Golf Course. I won't use names, but there was a big shot football player that thought his shit didn't stink and always picked on this one kid in class. Finally, the kid challenged him to a fight across the street on the Paramus Public Golf Course after school. It was a major deal, and word spread throughout the halls, and that was the place to be after school. The fight broke out, and the football player got the shit beat out of him. This bullied kid had so much rage built up inside he had superhuman strength, and that football player never bullied another kid after that! So stand up for yourself or stand up for those that can't stand up for themselves.

One day I was reading a bedtime story to my son, Johnny, when he was in first grade, and he looked really angry and scared, so I asked him what was wrong. He told me that this kid kept pushing him and bullying him. We alerted the headmaster of the school and made her aware of the child in question, but the bullying continued. So the New Jersey came out in me, and I told him the next time this kid pushed him, hit him as hard as you can right in the nose. So the next day, Johnny was pushed and then Johnny hit that kid right in the face! My wife and I were called into the headmaster's office later that day, and the headmaster said she is suspending Johnny for fighting. I told her the reason my son stood up for himself was because she didn't handle the situation. So if you suspend him, I'll take him to Sea World. So the day he was suspended, we had the best day ever, and that kid never messed with Johnny again. Sometimes you have to stand up to bullies to earn their respect.

The best way to use your words was when I was general manager of WILD 94.9 in San Francisco. We had a controversial morning show called *The Dog House*, and there was a reporter called Brad Cava from the San Jose Mercury News that always wrote not-so-nice articles about their show. I called Brad one morning and warned him that if he ever wrote another negative article about *The Dog House*, he would regret it. He asked me if I was threatening him, and I said, "Not physically, but I promise you won't be happy."

The very next day, he wrote another article about *The Dog House*, so I made good on my promise. If you are too young to remember *Mad* Magazine, had pages that when you folded it a certain way, it would say something totally different. So, my graphic artist, Stu Wyatt, created a half page ad that once you folded it, it was the middle finger and said "Fuck Brad Cava!"

I spoke to one of his coworkers the next day, and she said Brad's cubicle was full of "Fuck Brad Cava" ads! So as your parents taught you, use your words, not your fists...LOL. If all else fails you need to protect yourself.

The toughest kid in grammar school was Bobby Jones. I really liked the kid, but he challenged me to a fight before I started my paper route one afternoon. The rules were first blood wins. No, Sylvester Stallone didn't get the name for his movie from this fight... LOL. I took the first shot and gave him a bloody nose, and the fight was over! Not only did I earn his respect, but also word traveled, and nobody messed with me after that.

When I worked in Manhattan at WPLJ Radio, I often took a bus from the port authority bus station to get to my car on the Jersey side. One day, I was crossing the street, and this huge African American man was harassing a girl and was grabbing her arm.

I immediately grabbed her other arm and said, "Honey, come on. What you are doing?"

I walked her across the street. She thanked me profusely, and I told her it was my pleasure.

Sometimes, it takes quick thinking instead of force, but always try and use your words to talk your way out of a difficult situation or the best advice if you feel threatened is to run away as fast as you can!

Don't Make Excuses, Find Solutions

Anytime a salesperson or manager comes to me with a problem, I ask them what do they suggest we do to fix it. It was always easy going to your parents with problems, and they would give you a shoulder to cry on, but this is the real world, and you need to think for yourself. I hate excuses because excuses turn into lies, and I hate liars. Be proactive, not reactive. Think about what you would do before you go to your manager. Be a problem solver, not part of the problem!

Do the Things You Hate First

You will wake up almost every morning with a list of things you need to do, so my advice is, do the things you hate first! Your day will be so much happier and productive. Procrastination is a killer in the business world, so don't be afraid to make decisions, and get those tasks you are putting off first. I hate doing my taxes every year because I itemize, and it takes a long time. When I put it off, I think about it every day, and it weighs me down. When I do my taxes on time, I feel like a major weight lifted off my shoulders.

A Bad Decision Is Better Than Not Making One

In life, you'll need to make a lot of decisions, but being indecisive is a crippler. It is better to make a bad decision than not making one at all. You can fix a bad decision as long as you recognize it was one. Nobody likes to work for a person that is indecisive. Indecisive leaders lack followers! Weigh the pros and cons, and do what your gut tells you. We all make bad hires, so the key is don't put off their termination. They will do more harm to your business than by keeping them, and in some cases, it can cost you your job!

Hire People that Have the Skills You Lack

We have all heard, hire people that are better than you, but I think a better way to look at it is to examine your team and hire people that have different strengths: a good negotiator, a closer, an excellent writer, etc. (*Assemble a team that all have the same goal but different ways of getting there.*)

How to Terminate an Employee

Hiring is the fun part, but firing someone sucks! Most people I have let go see it coming, but there are occasional blindsides. I won't mention names, but one of my employees was known for stealing gift cards, etc., at our front desk that were supposed to be prize giveaways for listeners. I set up a sting operation to see if my employees that were suspicious of her were right. Wouldn't you know it? I had a video of her in the act of stealing the very next day and let her go immediately, she didn't even want to watch the video! This was allegedly going on for years, but I was new at these radio stations and got to the bottom of it in short order. That termination didn't hurt because that was a violation of trust. I called everyone in the conference room immediately after I let her go and said stealing is not tolerated here and mentioned how that person won't be here tomorrow.

My rule for terminating an employee is, get to the point, and get them out of the office. The meeting should last two minutes.

Never Bad-mouth Your Employer, Company, or Teammates

If you are miserable coming to work every day, then go find another job! People that are complainers are cancer, and once cancer spreads, you know the outcome. Loyalty is everything to me, and if it is ever violated, they are off the roster. If you can't trust your employees, then you don't have anything, and they are not on your team. My advice is, eliminate the complainers because they can bring your entire organization down!

I Wouldn't Want Dennis Rodman on My Team

There is no doubt that Dennis Rodman was a fantastic basketball player, but he was disruptive to the team and organization. In my eyes, he wasn't a team player because he was all about himself, and to me, I'd rather have a team full of excellent players than one outstanding one. It sends a bad signal to the rest of the players that this guy gets preferential treatment. I do believe certain people deserve special treatment, but they better be a team player as well. Love him or hate him, Tom Brady is an exception to the rule. Tom is the best quarterback that ever played the game and is a total team player, and that comes from me, a huge New York Giants fan…LOL.

Be Memorable

If you ever watch *America's Got Talent* or *American Idol*, judges are looking for acts and singers that are memorable and different. Vanilla doesn't work anymore. You need to be a specialist and offer something an employer can't get from anyone else or live without.

I was a pretty strong seller in Chicago, working at WLS, and my boss got mad at me one day and, in a sales meeting, said, "What do you want ten Bob Visotcky's sitting in this room?"

I had a huge smile on my face and said, "Would that be a bad thing? Imagine how great sales would be?"

The other salespeople were cracking up, but he wasn't so amused. I was a tough employee to manage, but I always treated my accounts and radio stations as if I owned it. I had a little Dennis Rodman in me but was a total team player.

I have always tried to come up with original radio promotions nobody else thought of. If the promotion was memorable, a revenue generator, and increased ratings, then we were going to do it. A few examples would be as I mentioned earlier in the book, attempting to make "Born to Run" the state theme song of New Jersey. Our radio station, WPLJ/NYC, made international news, and our ratings went up in New Jersey.

Another favorite promotion I came up with was musical cars, where people registered online, and we chose eleven contestants to play musical cars, like musical chairs, with the winner getting the last car in the ten-car line-up. We had a chair in front of each car and eliminated one car, one chair and one person until there were two people, one car, and after the final song stopped playing, we had our winner.

Here is one of my absolute favorites. I was driving home from a client call in Chicago, listening to Steve Dahl and Garry Meier doing their afternoon show on WLS/FM. It was about twenty-two degrees below zero that January day, and Steve and Garry had a woman from the Maui Marriott on the phone doing the weather report. Boom, an idea hit me, and it was a big one. "Picture Yourself in Hawaii." We chose ten of the most creative photos of people in Chicago in the dead of winter, dressing up like they were on the beach in Hawaii on the streets of Chicago in subzero weather. It was a huge success, and American Airlines and the Maui Marriott were my two initial sponsors. The following year, it was "Sing Yourself to Hawaii," and it was an even a greater success! If we played their one-minute song on the air, they had thirty minutes to call in and claim their trip for two to Maui.

When I worked in Charleston, West Virginia, we came up with the idea of naming the "Seven Wonders of West Virginia." That received a huge response from our listeners, and one listener won a trip to all seven wonders by registering online.

As automotive director for *The San Diego Union-Tribune* newspaper in San Diego, I had to lead a meeting of 105 salespeople and be the emcee for all the other department heads. It was Halloween week, so I dressed up like Bob Dylan and wrote and played on my guitar the "UT is a Changin" to the melody of "The Times They Are a Changin." It was hilarious, I received a standing ovation, and it was memorable! People still see me and said that was the greatest meeting they ever attended.

So be memorable!

Dating

Dating is not what it used to be in my early years! There are apps, matchmakers, etc., so be careful because the pictures and ages generally don't meet reality. Women have to cover their drinks at a bar when they use the restroom, and they should ask for a guy's last name so they can do a quick background check on social media. Two things that really bother me are that guys aren't walking on the outside of the street with their lady and don't open their car doors.

Treat a woman like a lady and always be respectful. No means no. I have two daughters and a son, and we made sure they were trained well.

Don't Reward Bad Behavior or Undeserved Behavior

Kids today can do no wrong, and that needs to change!

They get trophies when there is no clear winner. We say good job when they miss a tackle, etc. How are they going to learn if you don't point out the bad too? My eldest daughter, Demi, thanks me every day for teaching her to have a good work ethic and tells me how spoiled these millennials that work for her are. They get bored easily, want to keep moving around from job to job, and expect to be paid six figures right out of college.

News flash! *You have to want it!*

When I was hired as a salesman for WPLJ radio in New York City at age twenty-two, I made $24,000 my first year, and it cost me $34,000 to live and work there. I wanted it so bad that I have been making over six figures and beyond since age twenty-eight. Most people would have quit, but if you want something bad enough, you need to make sacrifices.

Today, millennials want everything handed to them with some exceptions! If they don't get promoted the first year, they leave and look for another easy way up.

Don't Think About Marriage Until You Are Twenty-Five Plus

I have asked hundreds of people what age they thought they had a handle on where life was taking them, and almost all said twenty-five. At twenty-five, you have a few good years of work under your belt, and now should look for that special partner. I know marriage is getting a lot of bad press lately but going alone isn't fun. When your significant other loves you unconditionally and can't live without you, then get on one knee or ladies, gladly accept. Two heads are better than one, and the bar scene in your fifties and sixties is no fun!

My Grandpa John's Advice

My grandparents were the best people on the planet, and I learned a lot from them. Gramps always woke up and kissed my Grandma Edee after his shot of rye! He always taught me to finish what I started no matter how bad the outcome. If you commit to something, see it through. He also always opened a car door for any passenger, man or woman. He taught me to walk on the outside of the street when walking with a female or child. Hold the door open for a lady and stand when they leave the table to use the restroom at a restaurant. Respect for women has been gone by the wayside with the younger crowd, and I'd like to see it return. My grandparents were old souls with excellent family values, and I have learned so much from them and miss them every day.

One of the key things they taught me was they gave all their grandchildren unconditional love. They weren't rich financially, but they had way more in love for their family, and that was more important.

My grandparents and mom were excellent listeners and never interrupted when I was speaking, a lesson we all should learn from.

Take Family Vacations / Dinnertime

My kids can tell you many stories from our annual vacations on Long Beach Island, New Jersey. My grandparents started the tradition many years ago and actually spent their honeymoon on Long Beach Island. It's my happy place, and maybe I will retire there one day.

Take lots of family photos every year.

Have a family Christmas card photo taken every year and do a recap of the past year's highs and lows that you can send to your family and friends.

Have a family dinner every night with no phones, laptops, or headphones on. Actually communicate and listen to each other. You'd be amazed what you would learn from people you thought you knew.

People that tell me they haven't taken a vacation in years don't get any sympathy from me. Vacations are critical for your mental health, your family, and your performance. After a vacation, you come back to work refreshed, and it's like rebooting one of your devices.

Never Take Your Family for Granted

My daughter was a student at University of California, Santa Barbara, and she was rushed to the emergency room. As soon as I heard the news, I immediately drove an hour to the hospital. The lesson here is, I told her the importance of family over friends.

I looked at Demi and said to her, "Your friends are a couple of miles away, and not one friend is here by your side."

She then realized that her parents and siblings are the most important people in her life. Teenagers put their friends first, but when the chips are down, your family loves you unconditionally, and you should never take that fact for granted.

Be Highly Optimistic

Entrepreneurs don't have the word *failure* in their vocabulary! They are "find a way" people and don't let anything or anyone get in their way. These people are hard to find, but they are out there. Those types of personalities elevate your game. Haters are always going to hate and tell you that your idea sucks or point out all the negatives. Optimistic people tell you how they are going to solve a problem, not cause a problem. They are also proactive versus reactive. I can't tell you how many companies are more interested in fixing a problem after it occurs rather than anticipate the problem before it exists! Most people aim for the middle instead of thinking big. There is less competition at the outrageous goals so be courageous and shoot for the stars! Remember, if you want anything bad enough, you can make it happen!

Scared Money Loses

I have to give my dad credit for this one! When he and I would go to the casino in Atlantic City, he always told me to go there with a winning attitude because scared money loses. I hear people saying I'm only going to lose $200…well, guess what, they probably did! We go and say we're going to win $10,000, and sometimes it happens! Scared money loses also applies to job search, dating, etc. If you think something isn't going to happen, you are playing with scared money! Sometimes you have to just roll the dice and take risks. You can ski more relaxed than tensing up. You golf better relaxed, etc.

NOW WHAT?

Don't Worry About Things You Can't Control

Ninety-five percent of the things you worry about don't happen! Google it! Do your best every day and let the cards fall where they may. Think of how much time you have wasted in your life on things that never happened. Live more, worry less!

A Ball Always Bounces Back Up When It Hits Bottom

When you are really down and I mean you think there is no way out, remember this saying; a ball always bounces back when it hits bottom. That line got me through the worst time of my life. My Listinglight invention went belly up in 2010 due to the real estate crash in 2008. I lost my houses; had to find a job away from my family; my wife left me; my dog, Duvers, died of cancer; etc. What got me through was me being the ball. I hit bottom, and now it's time to show myself and my kids it's time to bounce back! Quitting is easy. Finding a way out builds character. Most people in my situation would have felt defeated, but my son, Johnny, told me how proud he was of me for taking a risk and changing the real estate industry. I cannot tell you how amazing that made me feel. My eldest daughter, Demi, and youngest daughter, Sophia, were also very supportive. Taking an idea and making it a reality was an amazing feeling. We sold twenty thousand Listinglights in seven different countries, but I held it two years too long and couldn't recover from the 2008 real estate market crash.

Put End Dates on Yourself

Most goals should have an end date. If you don't achieve your goal on the date you said, then give yourself an extension, but always give yourself time to achieve a task. When you do that, things get done! It also takes procrastination out of the picture. You can inspire people with words, but words are no substitute for action!

Don't Talk About it… Do It!

How many times have you heard people say I'm going to do this and that and it never happens? You have to start something before you start talking about it! You control the effort you put in. *Don't expect great results if you lack the effort.* You always hear people saying can you help me with this? *Figure it out*! If you don't know something, Google is right there at your fingertips. Help yourself instead of looking for someone else to figure it out for you.

Get a Physical Checkup Every Year at the Same Time

Your health is the most important thing! Eat right, exercise regularly, and get enough sleep. It's really that simple, but we make excuses like I don't have the time, I'm tired, etc. Make time! Thirty-minute workouts should be part of your daily routine.

Go for an annual checkup every year! Preventive maintenance is the best. The biggest health problems you have today should have been handled immediately! At fifty, get a colonoscopy. Women, get breast exams regularly and book your annual physical today!

Handle One Task at a Time/Prioritization

People today have too much on their plate, and when you have too many things going on at once, you become paralyzed and nothing gets done. You start one thing and then say, "Well, I really need to get this thing done," and so on. Prioritize the situation and then clean your house one room or task at a time. When I was an EMT for the Garfield Volunteer Ambulance Corps in New Jersey, we learned there are five ways to die, and severe bleeders die first. So when you prioritize something, find your severe bleeding.

NOW WHAT?

Timing Is Everything!

When I invented Listinglight, a night-light for real estate signs in 2006, the real estate industry was on fire, and banks were lending money to anyone with stated income. What nobody saw was the real estate bubble bursting, and a lot of bad loans couldn't be paid back. In 2008, the crash happened. Homes went into foreclosure or short sales, and realtors stopped buying my product. We sold twenty thousand Listinglights in seven different countries, but the crash was a devastating blow. The lesson we learned was we were probably too late on the real estate gravy train, or additionally, we didn't know when to get out. Timing is everything! You have to predict what the next hot trends are and be first to market. Right now, the cannabis industry is booming, but if you are reading this now, it's probably too late for you.

Save For Your Retirement

As I said earlier, if you put 10 percent of every check you earn from twenty-two years old on, you probably can retire by forty-five to fifty. That money will keep on compounding, and before you know it, you are rich! Our life expectancy is rising, so with medical advances and cures to deadly diseases on the horizon, I say plan on a longer life expectancy than you think. Also, if you have an IRA or 401(k), put in the maximum the law requires.

Do Your Taxes on Time and Hire an Accountant

My accountant, Ron Ogulnick, not only is an excellent CPA but also a great friend and probably knows me better than most. He has seen me at the top, bottom, and middle and is always there for me. Hiring a professional is always the way to go whether it's doing your taxes, plumbing, painting your home, etc. You might save money doing it yourself, but that is not your expertise, and you probably will not do as good a job or fail miserably trying.

April 15 is tax day, and if you don't file, late penalty charges can go in effect. You can file an extension, but that doesn't get you out of paying interest on the money you may owe.

Do One Major Experience That Gets You Out of Your Comfort Zone Every Year

Here are some of mine that I actually accomplished:

- Be the best dad possible.
- Be a general manager of a radio station by age thirty.
- Buy a 450 SL Mercedes.
- Own my own home.
- Go to the top of the Eiffel Tower.
- Certified scuba diver and dive the Great Barrier Reef.
- Learn to surf.
- Run the New York City Marathon.
- Triathlete
- Skydive from 10,300 feet.
- Get my real estate license.
- Five-day Cataract Canyon whitewater rafting trip in Moab, Utah, with no phones or outside communication.
- Single-digit golf handicap.
- Start a foundation that helped people in need without the red tape of a corporation.
- Joined a fraternity (Phi Kappa Psi, WVU).
- Took martial arts in College.
- Visit Paris, Scotland, Germany, England, Australia, Belgium, and Greece.
- Write this book.

I did put an end date on each of these accomplishments with the exception of being a great dad, I couldn't predict my own death… LOL.

NOW WHAT?

Buy or Lease a Car?

My advice is, if you are going to buy a car, purchase a two-year-old car. The reason is you'll pay up to 50 percent less off the sticker price. When you drive a new car off the lot, try selling it the next day for what you paid, and they will laugh at you. You lose money the second you drive away from the new car dealership. Lease a car if you like changing cars every three years, and you don't drive a lot of miles. Since most cars depreciate 20 percent every year for the first four years, my advice is, buy a two-year-old car and drive it into the ground.

Buy Real Estate

My general rule about buying real estate is if you are planning to live in an area for five or more years, buy! If you do buy, find the best area and buy the cheapest house on the street. In real estate its location, location, location! Buying real estate is the best investment we ever make. If you buy right, you will make an amazing return in short order. People laughed at me when I bought a lot on the best street in Toluca Lake, California, for $910,000. It was Red Foxx's old home, and there were actually three structures on the lot. I hired a builder and built a 7,600 square feet home and all in, cost me $1,800,000. I sold it eighteen months later for $3.26 million, 81% return!

There is always a deal out there, but it takes time and research. I got my real estate license for two reasons:

1. I wanted to learn the industry.
2. When I bought my own homes, I could save commissions and negotiate the best price.

I would also recommend buying a multi-unit property that gives you a recurring revenue stream. You can live in one unit and rent out the others. The rent will pay the mortgage, and in time will make you money when you are ready to sell. If your kids are planning to go to college, buy a four-bedroom home, at their college and have one of your kids live in one room and rent out the others. It's a major tax right off, and when they graduate, you can keep it or sell it for probably a lot more than you paid. It might even be enough profit to pay for your kids' college education!

Recurring Revenue Stream Businesses Are Best

Think about it! Credit card companies make you pay interest on your balance every month. If you own property, you collect rent every month. If you have a dating site, you get customers paying you every month...you get the idea. If you want to be rich, find recurring revenue streams.

Make Friends with the Biggest Guy in the Room

My son, Johnny, loves this one! I told him that when I go to a bar or a place with a lot of people, I introduce myself to the bouncers and biggest guy in the room and make quick friends. I joke and say, "If anyone messes with me, do you have my back?"

They usually shake my hand while laughing and say, "I got you."

Being Stubborn Can Possibly Get You Killed

When I was sixteen, I went to Passaic, New Jersey, to see my girlfriend, Alice, march in a parade. I wasn't old enough to drive, and it was a Sunday afternoon when I walked to the bus station after the parade. We had no cell phones back then and guess what...the buses didn't run on Sundays! Here I am in one of the toughest cities in New Jersey, and the only way out was calling my dad. There was a pay phone at the bus station, so I called him and said please get here as quickly as possible because I have a bad feeling. I hung up the phone and wouldn't you know it, six African American men were walking across the street, and I prayed they kept on walking past the drug store on the corner. They walked past the drugstore, and I thought my nightmare was over. Man was I wrong! Ten seconds later, they came around the corner and formed a semicircle around me against the brick wall of the bus station. I was so scared my eyelids were shaking. They asked me for money, and I said I had a quarter when I really had fifty cents and a ten-dollar bill. One of the guys tried to reach in my pocket to see if I was lying, and I punched him right in the mouth. Oh shit. All hell broke loose, and I was getting punched in the face, kicked on the ground, and then miraculously, my dad showed up and tried to run a few of the guys down with his car. They ran away, and my dad looked down at me in the gutter and asked me if I was okay. I looked at my dad with a huge smile and showed him the crinkled $10 bill in my hand. My advice is, give them the money. After that incident, I took martial arts and said that will never happen to me again!

Tell Your Children to Introduce Themselves to Their Teachers the First Day of Class

Introduce yourself to all your teachers on the first day and create a relationship. People will call you a kiss ass, but if that gets you an A, so be it! If you are in college, this really helps, and I'll tell you why.

I went to WVU, and in a final physical science exam, I forgot a protractor and asked the girl next to me if I could borrow it when she was done. What I didn't know is that the professor was standing right behind me. He immediately wrote an F on the top of my paper and said to meet him in his office at 3:30 p.m. to possibly be expelled for cheating. For the record, I did not cheat but just asked to use her protractor when she was finished. I went to the professor's office at 3:30 p.m. and told myself, "You better form a great relationship quick."

I explained myself, but his college ring got my attention. I thought I saw Phi Kappa Psi on his class ring and immediately asked him if he was a Phi Psi. The professor answered in the affirmative, and my expulsion nightmare was over. He told me he was giving me a D in his class and to get out of his sight. That was the second time being a member of the fraternity got me out of trouble!

Be Creative

Who doesn't love a creative person? We are all given a gift, and it's our job to find out what it is. Can you sing? Write? Build? Etc. Find it, and go after it. I love watching an older person after they raised their kids, go after what they should have done from the beginning. Life gets in the way sometimes, and people get into their comfort zones and are afraid to explore their inner talents. It's never too late, so start today and find that inner talent and expose it to the world! Steve Jobs changed the world with Apple products that are everywhere and you can too!

My mind is always ticking, and I am always trying to find new ways of doing things. Always look for what is missing and fill the hole with your creative juices.

Your Mom

Send your mom a letter on *your* birthday, and tell her how much she means to you. I would even go one step further and send her a present on *your* birthday and thank her for the amazing life she has given you! You can never say I love you more, than to your mom!

Write a Letter to Each of Your Children the Day They Were Born and Read it at Their Wedding

God willing, I will be at all of my children's weddings, but in the case I'm no longer on this earth, they'll have a letter from their dad. In my letters, they will know how special they are from the day they were born. Enough said. I'm tearing up right now.

Teach Your Children Manners

Please and thank you are rare nowadays with the youth, and that is sad. Most young people feel entitled, and parents let them get away with anything. I called all my elders Mr. and Mrs. But now, it's Bob even if they are five years old. Guys don't open doors for girls. Guys don't walk on the outside of a street, and dinner dates and family restaurant visits are marred by cell phones and kids playing games on their tablets.

Communicate with Your Children Regularly

Let your children know that they can tell you anything and there won't be major consequences if they tell the truth. My kids always felt safe to tell their mom and me anything, and that is very healthy. We aren't very strict, but we know when to be the parent and the friend. Too many parents baby their kids and over parent. Disciplining your child is a very tricky subject. The best way I ever have seen disciplining a child were from my nephew Richie and his wife, Lexi. Whenever their son misbehaves, which is rare, they take him into a quiet room and talk it out calmly. My nephew Franklin is the most well-behaved child I ever met because he has excellent parents who love him unconditionally and always makes time for him.

Let Your Kids Live Their Own Lives

Our job as parents is to get them to age twenty-one, and the rest is up to them! You aren't them. They have their own interests. They have their own lives. They can ask for guidance, but they have to learn for themselves the lessons of life. It's not always going to be perfect. There will be hardships. They will make mistakes, but hopefully, they will learn from the experiences of life. I hardly ever helped them with their homework. It made them pay attention more in class and not rely on mom or dad for the answers to their homework.

Get Out of Debt

Debt is a killer, and it's so easy to get into. Credit card companies love when we max out our credit cards and pay high-interest rates. Buy what you can afford! It's that simple. Overextending yourself causes stress, anxiety, suicide, etc. Get counseling if you are in over your head and make a plan to get out now!

Buy What You Need Not What You Want

Material things are temporary gratifications. We may want that new car, but once we have it, we say to ourselves it wasn't that big a deal as I thought. We look for temporary fixes. When we are depressed, we shop or buy something that we think will make us feel better. The odds are we probably couldn't afford it and charged it, which puts us in debt. Buy what you need, not what you want, and you'll enjoy life a lot more.

Write Handwritten Personal Cards to Your Family and Friends

The best birthday, Father's Day, or Christmas gift I ever received from all three of my children was their handwritten cards. It wasn't on a Hallmark card. It was on a regular piece of paper and I cried after reading every one of them. Being a great dad is something I work at everyday and my kids know they are my priority. My advice is to write a handwritten note to your kids and tell them how they changed your life for the better.

There Is Always Light at the End of the Tunnel

No matter how bad a storm, there is always light at the end of the tunnel. Sometimes the tunnel is longer than you want, but keep pressing through, and you will see the light. Remember, giving up, making excuses, or blaming someone else never works. It happened, so deal with it and fight through the hardships. Life always throws you curveballs so deal with them and do your best to weather the storm.

You Aren't Always Right

We have all been around that guy or girl that thinks they know everything! If you are that person, let me be frank and let you know, you don't! There will be times in your life when you are positive you are right, and you'll find out there is someone smarter than you. Learn to listen to all the facts before passing judgement.

Go with Your Gut Instincts

I've given this a lot of thought, and I believe gut instincts come from experience. Based on what you have witnessed in your life thus far and you make decisions on your intuition. Sometimes it's a guess, but like I say, again and again, it's better to make a bad decision than none at all. If you don't swing the bat, you'll never get a hit.

Don't Look for Perfection in an Imperfect World

We all know people that are looking for what's wrong with a person before what's right with a person. Why is that? There aren't any perfect humans because we all have faults. Some people are never satisfied, and they keep searching until it's too late and die alone. It is so much better sharing your life with someone than being alone. Two minds are better than one, and we all need someone to listen to us, hug us, be intimate, and be best friends. We judge too much on first impressions and don't even give a person a chance to get to know them. The love of your life might have been swiped to the left, on a dating app, without you ever getting to know that person?

Enjoy Your Job

When I was in grammar school, our janitor, Mr. Carpenter, was always sweeping the floors, cleaning our toilets, picking up our vomit when we were sick but always with a smile on his face. He loved his job and loved the kids. Mr. Carpenter put me in a good mood every morning, and he always said, "Good morning, Bob!"

    A smile goes a long way nowadays, so smile more! If you don't like your job, quit and find one you like. There is nothing worse than hating to wake up and go to a job you don't like. If Mr. Carpenter can make his job enjoyable, then you should rethink how lucky you are.

Unemployment

I hope you never experience being fired or being unemployed, but I have tons of experience in both. The media industry changes often, especially ownership. With new ownership, management changes are almost certain. Getting fired is the worst! You feel like a failure. You question why they fired you, and you get really scared about what to do next. My best advice is, move on and don't try to justify why they fired you or bad mouth the guy or company that fired you. Probability is there is nothing you can do but move forward.

I worked my entire life in the radio industry to become market manager of six top producing radio stations in Los Angeles, billing about $250 million in revenue. One day, three weeks before Thanksgiving, my boss in Boston called me and asked me if I was sitting down.

I said, "What? Why do you care if I'm sitting down?"

The bottom line is he fired me on the phone after working seven years for that company and four promotions. My boss in Boston, Ken O'Keefe, didn't even have the decency to fire me in person or give me a reason. Our company was being bought by iHeartMedia so that was possibly the reason, but I'll never know. It took me five years to get over that, but it was wasted time and energy. You learn from your mistakes, and I learned that when you get bad news like being fired, pick yourself up, dust off, and get to work on the next opportunity. I moved to San Diego and started my own business.

Action Is the Cure for Procrastination

Start the process today. If you have an idea for an invention, want to write a book, become an actor etc. Start now!

Love Yourself First

You can't love anyone unless you love yourself. There are pleasers, and there are narcissists. You will live a much better life if you learn to balance your job and family. Most workaholics regret not spending more time with their families and friends. What good is money without happiness, so balance work with pleasure and love yourself. When I was general manager of WILD 94.9 in San Francisco, I invited my boss, Allen Shaw, to dinner with my family. After dinner, we walked to the Tiburon Ferry, and he looked at me and said how much he regretted not spending time with his children. He put work first and was jealous of what he just experienced at my home.

Don't Let Other People Define You Or Your Company

My best advice is, be yourself and never change for anyone. They either like you for who you are, or they don't. The first thing I see in relationships is one person trying to change the other person. If you find yourself changing into what someone else wants you to be, it's time to move on! When I worked in the media industry our competitors tried to position our radio stations how they saw it not like it actually was. So, my advice is never let the competition position your company.

Have an Open Mind and Be Flexible

Nobody likes people that always have to have it their way. We all know a few people that are like this, and they should know that there is always someone with a better mousetrap than them. I listen to all the facts and opinions before I make a final decision.

Dieting Is a Temporary Fix

I have been on many diets, but nothing works better than controlled portions and exercise. Thirty minutes out of your day to exercise should be mandatory in your daily routine. You can eat anything you want as long as it is not in excess. One bite of a piece of cake or candy satisfies your craving so just don't go overboard. One helping is better than two or three helpings at dinner time! You have to change your eating and workout habits. Also, weigh yourself once a week, and see if your changes are working.

Kids Want Hang Time

I remember getting into a conversation with some of my radio buddies when one of my friends said all kids want is hang time. You don't necessarily need to play catch or do physical activity. They just want your presence. That means no cell phones or distractions. It means being present and engaging with them. Ask them questions about school, their day, and problems they are having. Watch one of their TV shows, or take them to a movie they want to see.

Say Yes to Networking Opportunities

My ex-wife was great at always having something for us to do. I didn't want to go to half of the things she made me go to, but the moral of the story is that you never know who you are going to meet. More positive things happen if you go than if you sit at home and watch TV. Get off the couch and meet new people every chance you get.

There Is No Substitute for Hard Work

The odds of winning the Lottery or being CEO of a startup that's worth billions is probably not very high…LOL. Hard work does payoff, and nothing great in life comes without some pain, sacrifice, and hard work. My goal was to outwork, out think and be the most creative person in my field. I have been on thousands of sales calls, and I still critic myself after every call and remember what was good and fix what was bad or forgotten. There is always someone better than you are, but I always tried to keep it close…LOL. Jimmy de Castro was my idol in the radio business, and I tried hard to be like him. He let you do your job, was always in a good mood, was highly creative, and didn't mind spending money to make money. He also was a relationship specialist! Everyone loves Jimmy de Castro, and I thank him now for the magnificent influence he had in my life.

NOW WHAT?

Selling Begins with the Word No

If you are in sales, there is no greater feeling than turning a no into a yes! Anytime someone tells me they aren't interested or they don't need to market their business, I joke and say, "Since selling begins with the word no, I'm glad we got that out of the way." Then I proceed to sell them…LOL.

Integrity Is Everything!

My friend, Mo Moore, sent this e-mail to me, and I wanted to share it.

Story Number One

Many years ago, Al Capone virtually owned Chicago. Capone wasn't famous for anything heroic. He was notorious for enmeshing the windy city in everything from bootlegged booze and prostitution to murder.

Capone had a lawyer nicknamed "Easy Eddie." He was Capone's lawyer for a good reason. Eddie was very good! In fact, Eddie's skill at legal maneuvering kept Big Al out of jail for a long time.

To show his appreciation, Capone paid him very well. Not only was the money big, but Eddie got special dividends as well. For instance, he and his family occupied a fenced-in mansion with live-in help and all of the conveniences of the day. The estate was so large that it filled an entire Chicago City block.

Eddie lived the high life of the Chicago mob and gave little consideration to the atrocity that went on around him. Eddie did have one soft spot, however. He had a son that he loved dearly. Eddie saw to it that his young son had clothes, cars, and a good education. Nothing was withheld. Price was no object.

And despite his involvement with organized crime, Eddie even tried to teach him right from wrong. Eddie wanted his son to be a better man than he was. Yet with all his wealth and influence, there were two things he couldn't give his son. He couldn't pass on a good name or a good example.

One day, Easy Eddie reached a difficult decision. Easy Eddie wanted to rectify the wrongs he had done. He decided he would go to the authorities and tell the truth about Al "Scarface" Capone, clean up his tarnished name, and offer his son some resemblance of integrity. To do this, he would have to testify against the mob, and he knew that the cost would be great. So he testified.

Within the year, Easy Eddie's life ended in a blaze of gunfire on a lonely Chicago street. But in his eyes, he had given his son the greatest gift he had to offer at the greatest price he could ever pay. Police removed from his pockets a rosary, a crucifix, a religious medallion, and a poem clipped from a magazine.

The poem read:

> The clock of life is wound but once, and no man has the power to tell just when the hands will stop, at late or early hour. Now is the only time you own. Live, love, toil with a will. Place no faith in time. For the clock may soon be still.

Story Number Two

World War II produced many heroes. One such man was Lieutenant Commander Butch O'Hare. He was a fighter pilot assigned to the aircraft carrier Lexington in the South Pacific.

One day, his entire squadron was sent on a mission. After he was airborne, he looked at his fuel gauge and realized that someone had forgotten to top off his fuel tank. He would not have enough fuel to complete his mission and get back to his ship.

His flight leader told him to return to the carrier. Reluctantly, he dropped out of formation and headed back to the fleet.

As he was returning to the mothership, he saw something that turned his blood cold. A squadron of Japanese aircraft was speeding its way toward the American fleet.

The American fighters were gone on a sortie, and the fleet was all but defenseless. He couldn't reach his squadron and bring them back in time to save the fleet, nor could he warn the fleet of the approaching danger. There was only one thing to do. He must somehow divert them from the fleet.

Laying aside all thoughts of personal safety, he dove into the formation of Japanese planes. Wing-mounted fifty caliber blazed as he charged in, attacking one surprised enemy plane and then another. Butch wove in and out of the now broken formation and fired at as many planes as possible until all his ammunition was finally spent.

Undaunted, he continued the assault. He dove at the planes, trying to clip a wing or tail in hopes of damaging as many enemy planes as possible, rendering them unfit to fly.

Finally, the exasperated Japanese squadron took off in another direction.

Deeply relieved, Butch O'Hare and his tattered fighter limped back to the carrier.

Upon arrival, he reported in and related the events surrounding his return. The film from the gun camera mounted on his plane told the tale. It showed the extent of Butch's daring attempt to protect his fleet. He had, in fact, destroyed five enemy aircraft. This took place on February 20, 1942, and for that action, Butch became the Navy's first Ace of World War II, and the first naval aviator to win the Medal of Honor.

A year later, Butch was killed in aerial combat at the age of twenty-nine. His hometown would not allow the memory of this WWII hero to fade, and today, O'Hare airport in Chicago is named in tribute to the courage of this great man.

So the next time you find yourself at O'Hare International, give some thought to visiting Butch's memorial, displaying his statue and his Medal of Honor. It's located between terminals one and two.

So what do these two stories have to do with each other?
Butch O'Hare was Easy Eddie's son.

Sit on Major Decisions for Twenty-Four Hours

I am usually pretty good at making decisions, but some decisions should be contemplated overnight. If it's a major career change, buying a home, investment, major move, etc., twenty-four hours is enough time to weigh the pros and cons. *You can always change a bad decision, but you can't change a missed opportunity.* Think about it…

Your Business Card Can Make You Stand Out

The former General Manager of WEBN in Cincinnati, David Macejko, had a very difficult last name like mine, so on his business card, he had the phonetics for his last name. I thought that was an amazing idea, so I asked permission to use that idea, and he granted it. So the proper way to say my last name is (Vi sots ski). It is also a great conversation starter when you hand someone a business card and also makes you memorable!

Never Let Anyone Get in the Way of Your Career

The only person you should be loyal to is yourself! I can't tell you how many broken promises were made to me in my career, so I learned the hard way, and that is to be loyal to yourself and your family and company second. You also should never be harassed or talked down to. I have seen some nasty e-mails to some fellow employees that I would never tolerate, and in today's world, it's something that should be reported to HR immediately.

I heard this back in New York City when I was working at WPLJ, and they said I should have a "Fuck You Fund!"

Have enough money on hand for six months so if a boss or company isn't living up to your expectations…Leave. If a boss gets in your way find a way around him or her. Just because one boss doesn't see your unique qualities don't let that stop you or define you. You are in charge of your career so don't you ever forget that! Be yourself and don't let anyone change you. *Always get your deal in writing before officially accepting the position!*

NOW WHAT?

Do Volunteer Work

The best job I ever had I did for free! From the age of fifteen to twenty-one, I was an EMT for the Garfield New Jersey Volunteer Ambulance Corps. I would spend many hours riding in the back of an ambulance, helping people involved in car accidents, cardiac arrest, strokes, burns, etc. I have many stories, but there aren't enough pages in this book to do it justice. The point I'm making is volunteering feels fabulous. Helping others and giving back gave me more joy than me actually doing the work.

I did predict that there should be ambulance related TV shows and movies back in 1976. That year, I produced a movie called *Ambulance Call* with a cameraman from CBS TV in New York who was also a member of the Garfield Ambulance Corps. The Garfield Police Department helped us pull it off by pulling over and arresting a drunk driver after we patched up the victim he just hit with his car. To all the doctor, ambulance, emergency 911 TV shows…you're welcome!

Show Up Every Day

You never know what a new day brings, but it's important to show up and see what comes your way. When I was the first market manager for AM/FM in Denver, I was only there for one year when I got the call I waited for my entire career. My boss, John Madison, called and asked me to come to Los Angeles the next day and meet with him and the President of AM/FM, Jimmy de Castro. They booked me a room at the Four Seasons in Beverly Hills, sat me down, and promoted me to market manager of six top producing radio stations in Los Angeles. It was euphoric! I also ran into Howard Stern, Jackie the Joke Man, Robert Duvall, Elizabeth Hurley, Hugh Grant and Sporty Spice all staying at the Four Seasons that glorious weekend. Finally, the job I truly worked my ass for was a reality. All the moves I made with my family to multiple states and radio stations finally paid off, and that's because I showed up every day and never took my foot off the gas pedal. It didn't last too long because my company was sold shortly thereafter, but the point is I got there! If you show up every day, good things can happen.

Learn From the Past, Don't Live In It and Embrace Change

Will Rogers said, "Even if you are on the right track, you'll get run over if you just sit there."

It aggravates me to no end when I hear people on my staff say they don't like change. You have to always try new ways to do things better. You watch the Olympics because you want to see records being broken! The world is constantly changing, so you need to change with it. People tell me print, radio, and TV are dying, and my answer is no, they are all adapting to the digital age. Using traditional media like radio, print, TV, and outdoor with digital makes an unbelievable media mix. People need to hear your message eight to twelve times, and it used to be three times. Tradigital media is where traditional media meets digital media.

How Would You Like to Be Remembered?

What do you want your legacy to be? What would your children, family and friends remember about you? Everyone needs to ask himself or herself that question throughout their life, and if you occasionally don't like the course your life is taking…change it. We all have limited time on this planet so make the most of it. Make every day count. Never lose hope. Keep your family and friends close and communicate with them often. My grandparents and I sat on their front porch, and it was a great time to reflect on life.

So when I am old and sitting on my front porch in the sky, I want my children to know that I loved them more than life, extremely proud of the amazing adults they have become, and will always be watching over them. I hope my friends will say I was a good, honest man that always had a smile on my face, tons of energy, and lived life to its fullest. Sure, there were hard times, but that's life. I hope I am remembered that I died with my integrity and took no friendship

NOW WHAT?

or relationship for granted. I was fortunate to live in many different states and thank radio and the media industry for all the experiences it has given me. I hope I have inspired many people and made a difference in their life for the better. I always tried to be a good leader and provider for my family. This is how I hope to be remembered...

Thanks for listening.

About the Author

Born in Garfield, New Jersey, Bob Visotcky is a highly successful start-up and turnaround specialist primarily in the radio industry for the past forty years and now an author and motivational speaker. Bob has worked for major market radio companies such as ABC Radio, Jacor Communications, AM/FM Radio, Cumulus Media, Hispanic Broadcasting, and West Virginia Radio Corporation. He has worked at legendary radio stations such as WPLJ / New York City, WLS/ Chicago, KISS/Dallas, KLOS/KABC/KFI/KOST/KBBT, Los Angeles where he was also Market Manager for six top-rated Los Angeles radio stations overseeing six hundred employees and $250 million in revenue. Bob also was the inventor of the first night-light for real estate signs called The Listinglight, sold in seven countries worldwide. Bob is a high-energy, "get it done" type of leader, and his staffs all over the country have learned a lot from his experiences and teachings. Bob has spoken at college campuses and was inspired to write *Now What* because he didn't have the guidance for the real world after he graduated West Virginia University and entered the workforce. This book contains advice and guidance to prepare you for your first job and the challenges of the real world.

CPSIA information can be obtained
at www.ICGtesting.com
Printed in the USA
BVHW071244210521
607866BV00002B/390